I Gave You Each Other:

A Journey of Faith and Inspiration

Cindy Tornes

Kristen,

Be inspired!

Cindy

the Peppertree Press
Sarasota, Florida

Dedicated in memory of my mother,

Georgia Dimple Ward,

who gave me the foundation of faith

Dave, Greg, Patty, Mike and Alyson Stachura
Used with permission from Duncan Studio, Pittsford, NY

Acknowledgments

There are several people who must be thanked for supporting me during the process of writing this book.

First, my husband Neil, who has been my confidante, champion, editor, and constant source of encouragement. Without him and the freedom allowed by his two year international work assignment in London, this book likely would not have come to fruition. There are no coincidences!

To my children, Adam and Kelly, who give me such joy and have provided many wonderful opportunities for building faith.

To Mike, Alyson, Dave and Greg who have reached back into tender memories to provide this story.

To the FLOPS for their faith in me and the stories they contributed.

To Mark Hare and Kevin Flynn for their insight and pearls of wisdom regarding publishing.

To Ron Kenner and Tom Pucket of RKedit whose edits made the book sound "spot on".

And finally to my forever friend, K.C. Legg and her trusty laptop computer. Without her unwavering support, faith and remarkable email finds, Patty's personal journey could not have been told.

Introduction

I remember my affliction and my wandering, the bitterness and the gall. I well remember them, and my soul is downcast within me. Yet this I call to mind and therefore I have hope: Because of the Lord's great love we are not consumed, for his compassions never fail. They are new every morning; great is your faithfulness.

LAMENTATIONS 3:19-23

According to the Merriam-Webster's Collegiate Dictionary, the word change is defined as ". . . to undergo a modification of . . . to become different, or . . . to undergo transformation, transition, or substitution."[1] We know how we would respond to positive changes, but do we know what our reaction would be to life changes such as illness or the loss of love, money or home that can actually cause one to struggle? Varying emotions are pulled from deep within us for these scenarios. The manner in which we deal with these feelings is frequently the key to the outcome. Our personality traits, past experiences and faith play a definitive role in our reactions.

In her book, *Scarred by Struggle, Transformed by Hope*, Joan Chittister explains that "to struggle is (to) begin to see the world differently. It gives us a new sense of self. It tests all the faith in the goodness of God that we have ever professed . . . It leads to self-knowledge. It builds forbearance . . . If we are willing to persevere through the depths of struggle we can emerge with conversion, independence, faith, courage, surrender, self-acceptance, endurance, purity of heart, and a kind of personal growth that takes us beyond pain to understanding."[2]

At first glance it will appear that this book is simply dealing with struggle since the main character is afflicted with ALS (amyotrophic lateral sclerosis) also known as Lou Gehrig's disease or Motor Neuron Disease in Europe and the UK. Patty Stachura faces a slow but inevitable death. Indeed, it reveals horrific struggle; but you will also come to see that it is also about hope, love and service. The story reflects the physical, emotional and spiritual journey during her battle with ALS as well as the journey of the friends who cared for her. It will leave you asking, victim or victor?

Once it was determined that Patty needed assistance in coping with her ALS, a group of friends joined together to volunteer for this purpose. We decided a name for the group was needed and the result was The FLOPS – Friends and Loved Ones of Patty Stachura. Each individual who became a FLOP brought something unique to her relationship with Patty. Some were nurses, past and present, others were longtime friends and some were new friends that she met through the Church of the Transfiguration and religious retreats to Booneville, Kentucky. They were an inspiration but they also were inspired. I want to introduce you to these key people so that you have some background as they are brought into the story.

1. **K.C. Legg** was a longtime friend of Patty's. They had met when both daughters were involved in soccer around 1995. They became "re-acquainted" and closer friends after Patty's first trip to Kentucky on retreat. She was one of Patty's dearest friends and confidantes, and was often engaged in decision making. K.C. brought strength and unwavering faith to the relationship.

2. **Peggy Brizee** and her husband Peter had been friends with Mike and Patty since the Stachura's move to Pittsford. Their sons played hockey together. Initially, she was probably Patty's first (and only) real friend. In the beginning of Patty's illness, Peggy brought compassion and concern to decision making when it became clear that she needed

assistance. Because of their personal history and friendship, Patty was open to her suggestions.

3. **Eileen Bieter** was Patty's sister-in-law. She was adamant that she wanted to be involved in the group despite not knowing the others and not living in Pittsford, because she and Patty had a special relationship. Eileen's visits were punctuated with laughter and innocence as Patty's young nephew Matt and sometimes her niece, Margaret, joined in the day. It was such a welcome and uplifting distraction for Patty and she looked forward to their visits.

4. **Cindy Tornes** (author) first met Patty on retreat in Kentucky in 1999 despite living in the same neighborhood. Whether it was due to my close proximity, nursing background or ability to be forthright, Patty dubbed me the "Major FLOP" and put me in charge of the group. I believe that I brought organization, practicality and knowledge. Patty shared her most intimate concerns and fears with me knowing she would sometimes get an honest and sometimes a sarcastic reply.

5. **Lynn Klotz** met Patty through church. Lynn, with her outgoing and outspoken personality brought many things to her relationship with Patty. She was a wonderful shopping companion helping Patty pick out future and current gifts for the kids. Lynn contributed to the group by introducing the importance of music to worship and friendship. This was a consistent, cohesive factor for the FLOPS and a continuing comfort for Patty. One meaningful song she introduced was Randy Travis' "Keep Your Lure in the Water."

6. **Allyson Bailey-Farchione** met Patty for the first time on a Kentucky Women's retreat. Her first "intimate" moment with Patty cemented the relationship. Allyson became a secure confidante for Patty and vice versa. Tears, laughter, and empathy were shared by both regarding the difficult trials they had been dealt.

7. **Joan Lienhardt** knew Patty from church. Joan was active

as a FLOP in the beginning when caretaking was minimal and the FLOPS were needed to keep Patty safe and provide social support. During the course of Patty's illness, Joan had to reduce her involvement due to her own health issues, but her role as a prayer warrior for Patty was unfailing.

8. **Susan Caselli** met Patty through the Kentucky retreats and became a loyal and committed friend. She was a good listener for Patty and an eager and consistent force in providing immeasurable encouragement and help in any way needed.

9. **Beverly Young** was a delight to Patty's heart. Her support and upbeat demeanor always gave Patty a lift or a laugh. Plus in Patty's eyes, no one came close to being the accomplished cook that Bev was.

10. **Jennifer Altier** was an active part of the prayer group that formed after her trip to Kentucky with Patty. She had total conviction in how Kentucky and Patty bonded the FLOPS together and she cemented this by introducing the song "I Gave You Each Other" by Bob Schwartz.

11. **Karen Fain Nowlan**, as the Transfiguration leader for many of the Kentucky retreats, came to know Patty well. She brought her keen intuition of unspoken spiritual needs to the friendship and was an empathetic listener. Her compassion was frequently shown in "the patting of the hands."

12. **Jo-Ellen Eckel** was an extremely compassionate FLOP showing utmost attention to the care and dignity that Patty needed. Her upbeat, but mild demeanor had a calming effect on Patty.

13. **Ann Smith** always had a knack for perking up Patty's spirit by doing little things to make her feel special and feminine – manicures, pedicures or tweezing her eyebrows. Ann knew what would help Patty feel better about herself.

14. **"Sis" Martin** knew Patty through their sons, Adam and

Dave, who were friends from high school into adulthood. Patty and Sis were able to share information, stories and gossip which kept them closer to their sons in Boston. Sis' marvelous sense of humor always made the visit pleasant.

15. **Becky Pronko** lightened Patty's burdens with her many stories that would keep Patty laughing and re-telling them days later. Trips in the van with Becky always left Patty a little breathless! Becky's experience with hospice also gave her much insight into Patty's needs.

16. **Carol Finucane** joined the group after Patty was confined to her wheelchair and her speech was deteriorating. Yet, Patty felt a special closeness to Carol who always was able to calm her spirit with her presence and touch. Carol's outward enthusiasm for life made Patty's days more enjoyable.

Honorary FLOPS

17. **Connie Wahl** would often visit between trips to Indianapolis where her new husband resided. Patty and Connie went together on many of the Kentucky retreats. Connie would have Patty in hysterics with her everyday antics and stories from her farm days, especially stories of Mary and Joseph her pet chickens.

18. **Cindi Newman** came to know Patty through the prayer group and providing meals. Patty was in awe of her biblical knowledge and her unwavering faith in the face of personal trials.

19. **Barbara Swiecki** was the pastoral associate who introduced Patty to Kentucky the first years of the retreat. Barb was instrumental in Patty's journey to a stronger faith and trust in God, as well as giving us the symbol of the cardinal to reinforce that trust. Patty was continually in Barb's prayers and Patty was aware of her commitment.

Together, this group became a lifeline for Patty and her husband Mike, and to each other as well.

Chapter 1

But the Lord said to Samuel, "Do not consider his appearance or his height, for I have rejected him. The Lord does not look at the things man looks at. Man looks at the outward appearance, but the Lord looks at the heart."

1 SAMUEL 16:7

As she lay sprawled on the ground in the dress she had bought for Alyson's (Aly) graduation from William Smith College, all Patty could think about was how embarrassed she was and how she wished the ground would just swallow her up. I can hear her thinking: "Look at these people staring at me! What a klutz they must think I am and boy are they right! This damn knee just seems to give out; all I did was stoop down to take a picture! How can I be so clumsy?" This was a slow motion replay for Patty, the second time in seven months she had fallen without warning.

The first time Patty fell she was a member of our 2002 'Walk for Diabetes' team, the Cardinal Crew. The group had walked together for several years to support family and close friends with diabetes. Patty had separated from the rest of the group and was rambling along chatting with Connie Wahl, another team member. The next thing she knew she was on the ground, with Connie flitting around trying to help. In retrospect, she wasn't sure why she had fallen but thought that she had caught her toe in the uneven sidewalk. Embarrassed and banged up, she was not really hurt. She let the ambulance take her back to the starting point of the walk; however, she absolutely refused emergency care. Patty, a nurse, knew she was fine and could take care of herself! Always the model of independence, she did not want to draw more attention to the situation. Most of the team only heard about the incident at the end of the walk. Now her knee had given out at Aly's graduation.

Little did Patty know that this embarrassment would not be the last. Later that month, May 2003, the family was gathered in Boston for Dave's graduation from Boston College. This time they were walking down the sidewalk to dinner when, without warning, she fell. She broke her glasses, scraped her face on the concrete and injured her knee; it swelled so badly she couldn't fly to Kentucky the next day for the Transfiguration Women's Retreat in Booneville. She blamed this incident on the rain and wet leaves on the sidewalk; however, with this third episode she knew she needed to see her doctor and have her knee checked out. In analyzing these falls, she realized that recently she had not been able to lift as much weight with her leg during her daily workouts at the YMCA.

This was baffling, as Patty had been working extremely hard to improve her health over the past year. She had joined Weight Watchers and saw continual success; no minor accomplishment. She was aware she had latent issues with food. As she confessed in her writings, *"I stuffed my emotions with food."* But Patty also loved to eat! She enjoyed the food, the sharing, the companionship, and the conversation. She was passionate about eating out and breakfast was one of her favorites; she was always eager to try a new diner, café or hole-in-the-wall restaurant. Sunday mornings after Mass were reserved for Forest Hills, a small diner/restaurant in East Rochester, New York. Forest Hills was just another small town restaurant with multiple booths and a back room of tables. Daily specials were posted on a large dry ink board overhead. Its claim to fame came to be the 2006 "WHAM 101.3 Tony & Dee's Best Fish Fry in Rochester Award." All the waitresses knew Patty by name and always knew what she wanted: Chocolate Chip Pancakes with sugar free syrup and a small orange juice. Yes, you read that right. She knew exactly how many Weight Watcher points were in those pancakes and yet, come hell or high water, she was going to have them! But she did not just begin devouring those fluffy light pancakes with the melted chocolate chips oozing out. Oh no, she had to artfully cut and prepare them first. This practically involved a geometry lesson as she cut off the edges to make a perfect square, then sliced through them in a pattern similar to a tic tac toe board. The edges were not to be eaten as this would have increased the Weight Watcher point allowance and, besides, the soft centers were the delicacy.

As part of the Weight Watcher Plan (or maybe because of the pancake indulgence), she had religiously been working out at the YMCA; swimming, using the treadmill and the upper and lower body weight machines, and slowly increasing the time and resistance. She also took long walks with K.C. Legg and me along the Erie Canal in Pittsford.

The three of us tried to solve all of our parenting worries during those afternoons in the sun. And over a year's time Patty was seeing her success, a weight loss of eighty pounds plus improved muscle tone. She was proud of her fortitude and her success and also found an unexpected result, the empowerment of her self image and self esteem.

During her first years in Pittsford, Patty would likely have scored herself a negative 10 on a self image scale. She and her husband Mike, along with their three children, Dave, Alyson and Greg moved to Pittsford in March 1992. Pittsford, a suburb of Rochester, NY, is known for its excellent school system and middle or upper middle class residents. Many people choose this area for the schools and the standard of living; many others refer to Pittsford as being snobbish, *"Oh, they live in Pittsford"*. Patty was not a fan of what she called the Pittsford mentality of *"Pittsford Perfect."* She never believed she fit into this community. Overweight, she did not think she looked the part. Nor did she feel she had anything in common with the mothers and women she met.

Patty and Mike started working with a counselor in 1995, and this periodically continued throughout the years. Quotes from Patty's undated journal (Assignment #6) reveal her feelings of inadequacy: *"Since moving to Pittsford, I've never had such an intensity around who I am (and) how fat I am. I am self conscious everywhere I go. I am uncomfortable in my own body. This is always, constantly on my mind, it never leaves."* Her journal also reveals an assignment (Assignment #1) that evidently had her list her fears and failures. This list, quoted below, was significant in focusing on her self esteem. But what is really astounding was #4, which seemed out of context, although it could have been in relation to her weight.

1. *I have failed to lose weight.*
2. *I failed to listen to my gut......*
3. *I am insecure.*
4. *I am afraid of dying too soon.*
5. *I am afraid to take a stand for fear people won't like me.*

Mike told me, "She was very concerned that she did not fit the Pittsford stereotype. I think in some respects she really thought she wanted to, but came to realize that she still needed to be herself."

One of the first Pittsford friends Patty made was Peggy Brizee. Peggy explains, "Patty and I originally met through Dave and Truman's love of hockey and other sports. I think I was probably one of her first and only friends right after she and Mike moved here from Orchard Park. She definitely missed her buds back home; and her mother especially. Our families got to know each other fairly well through our kids; no surprise there, and I know that Patty fully valued our friendship as did I. We didn't socialize very much but Patty and I nevertheless spent a lot of time communicating, mostly Patty phoning me with the latest news or crisis! There was always something going on with someone in the Stachura household upon which Patty had to act or vent! She didn't mince words but for a time I think I was her only female confidante. She allowed me to share her hopes and frustrations, right up to the last. What an honor..."

Patty's relationship with her children might be portrayed as a "mama bear with her cubs." She disciplined them since she realized they were not infallible; however, if she knew that they had been wronged, she would defend them to the end, even if it went against Pittsford norms.

Patty might be described as having a strong, controlling personality, as alluded to by Peggy. In some situations such as Patty's nursing profession this could be a positive attribute, but in social situations it could also lead to difficulties with personalities similar to hers. In addition to working with Sybil, Patty also began seeking some spiritual answers. Raised and married in the Catholic faith, she had a solid foundation to begin this search and she recognized that her counselor could not address that need in her life.

Chapter 2

*In my anguish I cried to the Lord, and he answered by
setting me free. The Lord is with me; I will not be afraid.
What can man do to me?*

PSALM 118:5, 6

Peter said to Jesus, "Lord, it is good for us to be here. . ."

MATTHEW 17:4

Patty and Mike attended the Church of the Transfiguration
with their children. Patty would be the first to tell you
she was not a person of unwavering faith. Since the death of
her mother which had left her feeling even more alone she
recognized she was a bit angry with God over this event,
and she was doing much soul searching. She also suffered
some guilt over a personal experience that she couldn't get
beyond. This, coupled with her feelings of social unaccep-
tance, were valuable topics for her counseling sessions.

In 1998 Transfiguration offered a retreat for women to
work with the poor in Booneville, Kentucky; it was led by
Barbara Swiecki, the pastoral associate. Owsley County,
with Booneville as the county seat, remains one of the

poorest counties in the United States. Statistics by the U.S. Census Bureau in 2008 stated that 37.6 percent of individuals lived below the poverty level and the median household income was $19,829.[3] There is no industry; alcoholism, abuse, poverty and drugs are rampant and the people are fiercely independent, not looking fondly on "outsiders".

In the midst of this desolation is a mission Catholic Church, The Church of the Holy Family, led by Sr. Marge Eilermann with the help of Sr. Karen Lindenberger. For several years, the Men's group from Transfiguration had been spending a week in September working with the poor, and Barb felt this would be an awesome experience for the women of the parish as well. The work would include painting, cleaning, repairs, and whatever else was asked to be done by Sr. Marge. Another aspect of the work included kitchen table ministry. This involved a group member spending time talking with a person to hopefully form a relationship. We call it ministry, although it does not mean that we specifically talked about religion. It was more a sign of caring.

Barb encouraged Patty to go that first year but to no avail. Patty was too unsure of herself to become an intimate part of a group of fifteen women. In 1999, K.C. Legg was attending for the second year and asked Patty to go. With both K.C. and Barb nudging her, she decided to participate. Mike was very supportive as he recognized that Patty was spiritually searching for a connection to God and to other women. By this time, Sr. Marge was no longer at the mission but was serving time in prison for trespassing on the School of the Americas during a peaceful demonstration. She was replaced by Sr. Bea Herman, a 75 year old spitfire. Patty was very hesitant about this trip, since she strongly felt that these Pittsford women would be judgmental and non-accepting of her; a general theme in her retreat journals. Little did she know how life altering this experience would prove to be for her.

Patty expressed her misgivings in her journal writings the first two retreat days: (Saturday) *"This is very hard for me. I called Mike, I just needed to hear his voice (and have) some reassurance that I did the 'right thing' by coming along."* Mike told me later that he thought she was going to be on the next plane home, it was that intense! (Sunday) *"We had a prayer service in the morning; it's hard for me to get used to praying with other people in a small group setting. Sometimes it's just hard for me to pray and have faith. I still am a little angry with God as to why he took my Mom. I want things to go well this week, I realize that everyone here will not be my best friend, but I want to be accepted for who I am, not what I look like. Some of these ladies are not leaving the 'air' of Pittsford at home. It's so much a part of them; I realize they can't see it. I hope I don't act that way . . . I do pray this trip (helps) in my search for what seems to be missing in my life. I need to worry less and put more trust in God that things will be OK. I really have to trust God again, (I have to) find a way to do that."* This last sentence was highlighted.

Monday brought the first day of work for the group. Patty was foreman of her work group and prayed for the strength to be kind and patient. Ultimately she was very proud of herself. Patty's journal description of the home they worked on reads: *"(The man) looked to be about 60 but in reality is probably in his late 40s, his health is bad and he moves slowly. At first, they were not really excited for us to be there. It's hard to let someone into your home (and) ask for help* (how insightful this would be later); *but I think they knew they needed the help. The kitchen had grease like I've never seen before, there were cockroaches and the cooking utensils were beyond what a human should be eating from. The sparseness of the kitchen really struck me. I think of all we take for granted in this life. They had a gas stove, a refrigerator from the 1950s, I would guess, a tiny microwave, no kitchen cupboards, just a sink and a steel four-shelf rack to store food and tools on, and a kitchen table and chairs. There were probably only three shelves of food and not much in the refrigerator. It was amazing (for three people). I think I am beginning to feel some of the lost feelings I used to feel about God and his presence. I know He was there watching over us today; as we left I felt good about how much we had accomplished. I had fun, and I felt I handled myself pretty well, even though I had thought I wouldn't be able to do it. Then a beautiful cardinal flew by in front of the car as if to say, 'Well done ladies, thank you. And Patty you did well.' One more thing, I believe God sent Mom to be with me, to help me part way through the morning. I was outside and a yellow butterfly fluttered around the yard and flew away. Thanks Mom for guiding me and helping me. Thanks God for sending my mom to me. It gives me a warm, comfortable feeling and completes a part of my soul I miss so dearly.*

Tuesday was a terrible day. Things came to a head with me and three people. They perceived me as abrupt, not caring and too goal oriented; some of them want to talk and so they feel inadequate because I do my work faster than them. I tend to people on a daily basis. I don't want to do it here. I needed to come here to work, talk a little, and leave the Pittsford world behind. I went to two of the people on my own. I cried and cried as they told me how they felt, and we talked about my feelings and all the misinterpretations that occurred throughout the day. It felt good and I believe all the tensions are out and we all feel better about things."

On Thursday, Patty was to read the Gospel and give the homily (a talk reflecting on the Gospel message). Wednesday night she tried to write a homily and spilled many of her true feelings into this rough draft. "*In today's Gospel, Jesus came with the message that God loves us unconditionally. He also tells us that he simply wants us to live in unity, to be one with Him. The last few days have been very powerful, in fact, overwhelming at times. Besides serving the needs of the people of Boonville, one of my main reasons for coming here was to leave the 'Perfect Pittsford' world behind, to find unity, to find a circle of people to accept me for me – not to judge me for how I look, or dress, or what kind of car I drive. But also to find my 'way back' to a stronger faith, a faith I used to have growing up. My faith in God has been tested.*"

Ultimately Patty decided not to use this version. "*I did the homily today, which was a new and different experience. I tried to write one but instead I just winged it. I talked about Mom and how important she was to our family and was the one who held us together as one (referring to the passage John 17:11, 12 where Jesus refers to the disciples as being united). My partner and I who were on kitchen crew then went to visit one of the houses – cockroaches, spiders, a pack of dogs, and gun shots! I will miss these girls; it has truly been the best thing I could have done and I will treasure it always. I already want to come next year.*"

Patty did go that next year, and for two other years, and she drew strength from these retreats. She felt God's presence in the nature around her and especially when she saw a cardinal. On the first retreat Barb had told us the significance of cardinals in her own life. When she saw them, she felt God's nearness and knew that worries would be taken care of. As the leader, Barb was very anxious about how things would go on the first Kentucky retreat. However, when she drove out of her driveway to meet the ladies at Transfiguration that morning, she saw a cardinal which calmed her fears. Some of you will likely doubt the power of cardinals, but over the years there have been multiple problems I have encountered that were suddenly resolved after such a sighting. As we caravanned to Booneville, cars got separated and lost contact (before cell phone use) in the rush hour traffic of Cincinnati. While the lead car waited at an exit, a cardinal was seen and within 30 minutes the rest of the group arrived unknowingly at the same exit. Another time while replacing carpet in a Booneville home, we unknowingly moved a gas heater and then smelled gas. Obviously we called the gas company but also spied a cardinal while waiting. The repairman who arrived had the initials J.C. on his uniform. K.C. still talks about Jesus Christ coming to fix the gas leak! In Pittsford, I had never noticed a cardinal in my neighborhood during the seven years we lived there. We had received some worrisome news from the doctor regarding our daughter's lab tests. As I drove down a street close to our home, I was crying and praying when suddenly a cardinal flew in front of the car and immediately I felt a sense of peace. Ultimately the medical workup showed there was no health concern. To some these may seem like occurrences of random chance; but to women who have been on a Kentucky retreat, upon seeing a cardinal we feel God's presence.

On our return to Pittsford, Barb always gave a reflection at Sunday Mass at Transfiguration. During her year

2000 reflection, she quoted St. Ignatius of Loyola's prayer that points God's people in the right direction. "Teach us, good Lord, to serve thee, as thou deserves, to give and not to count the cost, to fight and not to heed the wounds, to toil and not to seek for rest, to labor and not to ask for any reward, save that of knowing we do Your will." Barb's reflection continued: "We learned what the prayer means. We learned that we can't trust ourselves; we need to trust Jesus and to look to him for guidance. We learned that we are not in control; that our own agendas really aren't important. We learned that we can't fix everything, and sometimes what we perceive to be broken doesn't need fixing at all."

Kentucky was a place where Patty knew without doubt that she was learning to trust. She felt drawn to God, to the people of Booneville, to the nuns at Holy Family Church, and to the Transfiguration women who accepted her and became true friends. I tried to capture our spirituality in a poem written after returning from the 1999 retreat.

TEN CAME TO THE MOUNTAINS

"Come to the mountains"
The Lord said to ten.
"I need you to model,
And be fishers of men."
And so to be faithful
The ten headed forth,
To work with the families
To show them God's worth.
We came to serve others,
A ray of God's light.
However not knowing
We'd find great insight.

Our clothes, hats, and hands,
Were dirtied and worn.
But our love for the Lord
Was rekindled, reborn.
For love produces love,
And God uses each one
To carry out His mission
Until His work is done.
So thank you, Our Father,
For the blessings received,
For bread that was broken,
And friendships conceived.

Chapter 3

In his heart a man plans his course,
but the Lord determines his steps.

PROVERBS 16:9.

In the early spring of 2003, life was good for Patty. She was feeling positive about herself. She had developed a close friendship and was spending time with K.C. Legg and myself. She and Mike were successfully coping with empty nesting with the children in college and heading off to jobs, and she was cultivating her relationship with God. Mike finished his application for the Permanent Deaconate for the Catholic Church in May. Patty had a nursing job in employee health at Thompson Hospital in Canandaigua, N.Y. that she found stimulating and she had fostered a friendship with Juanita Marshall, a co-worker. Since her life seemed to be turning around, she was frustrated with the possibility of a knee problem that might sideline her.

She went to see her Primary Care Doctor who examined her and ordered a scan which did not show anything definitive for the knee giving way. He suggested physical therapy which she agreed to, but ultimately did not see any significant strengthening when she was at the gym. In early summer she noticed some other mysterious things occurring in her body: twitches in her right biceps and difficulty turning the ignition key on her Explorer. She began researching her symptoms on the internet and voiced concerns to K.C. and I about neurological diseases. Her remedy was to push herself harder at the gym. Having had experience as a neurosurgical nurse, I told her it most likely was some sort of nerve compression and that she was getting overly concerned.

I couldn't fathom that it was something serious. I can distinctly remember the day my laissez faire attitude changed. We had just returned from a walk and were sitting in her driveway when she looked at me, tears welling in her eyes, and told me that she was pretty sure she had ALS. I thought to myself, "Here we go again. She is really off the deep end," and almost rolled my eyes! But as a good friend and nurse should do, I instead probed her reason for saying this. She relayed the symptoms she had read about and the symptoms she had, pointing out the muscle fasciculation in her arm. She then showed me the palms of her hands and I was astonished at what I saw. Where normal muscles are plump and full in the palm, hers were concave and wasted away. No wonder she was having trouble with her car keys. She might actually be making some sense with her deductions about a neurological disease, but ALS still seemed a stretch. I also got teary and emphasized that she needed to go to the doctor again. I remained a skeptic, even though my subsequent internet research indicated wasting of the palms was a later sign of ALS. Patty had truly diagnosed herself.

She finally took her concerns to her doctor who referred her to a neurologist. Multiple tests were done throughout the summer, most of which only eliminated or ruled out diseases. By this time she was also having some foot drop issues in her right foot and was using a cane intermittently due to her fear of falling, since this could occur without warning. K.C. recalls sitting with her one evening while Patty talked about how scared she was and how she was afraid of what lay ahead for her. They decided to use the Angel cards that K.C. had discovered at her massage therapist's office. Patty randomly drew the Archangel Michael card with the following text:

Card meaning: This powerful archangel is with you right now. He gives you courage and helps release you from the effects of fear.

Through this card, Archangel Michael is making his presence known to you. He is the symbol of true courage, stemming from knowing that God's love is the only power there is. Michael is letting you know that as you make changes in your life and as you encounter challenges, you are safe and secure. God and the angels help you stay true to yourself during trying times.

Have heart–to–heart discussions with Michael often. Pour out all of your concerns to him. Don't worry about overburdening him. Michael, like all of the archangels, is able to be with everyone simultaneously who needs him. He has no limitations of time or space, so he can help you and others concurrently.[4]

Was this card drawn by accident at this point in time? I do not believe so. Five years later, while touring Moscow, I was reminded of the Archangel Michael when our tour guide discussed the religious icons of the Russian Orthodox Church, which has many similarities to the Catholic faith. She explained that the Archangel Michael is the first angel to greet us as we enter heaven. Psalm 56:3 reminds us, "When I am afraid, I will trust in you." I firmly believe that God's hand was at work.

Finally in August, the neurologist, in a very matter of fact way, told Patty and Mike that he had ruled out everything else; that he felt Patty likely had ALS and that there was nothing that could be done. Talk about devastation! She could not believe how callous he acted. In September she met with Dr. Charles Thornton, a different neurologist who specializes in ALS at the University of Rochester's Strong Memorial Hospital. Quite the opposite of the first experience, Dr. Thornton showed extreme concern and compassion for Patty and Mike's reactions to this overwhelming news. With this information, Mike withdrew his application for the Catholic deaconate.

Amidst this difficult time, I felt guilty as I left to live in England where my husband was living on a work assignment. Patty was struggling and I was touring Europe. K.C. felt the brunt of this, but all I could do was light candles and pray for her in every cathedral we visited in Europe.... She had candles burning all over the continent! When the assignment unexpectedly ended in December and we returned to Pittsford, I was astounded at the increased weakness that had occurred over those three months. During this period, Dr. Thornton continued some further testing and she was fitted for a leg brace to help with the foot drop.

This involved wearing black orthopedic shoes which again wreaked havoc on her self image! He confirmed the diagnosis in December 2003 and Patty and Mike were quickly linked with the ALS division of the Muscular Dystrophy Association for support. At Patty's request, she was also referred to a specialist in NYC at Columbia Presbyterian Hospital. In January, he reconfirmed the diagnosis. She soon began taking Rilutek, the only drug which had been found to be somewhat effective against ALS.[5]

As anyone would be, Patty was inconsolable. She went through a myriad of emotions each day: anger, grief, pity, bargaining, disbelief, worry, shock, feelings of unfairness and fear. All K.C. and I could do was listen. She worried about telling Dave, Aly and Greg, knowing how devastated they would be. A mother was supposed to be the protector and yet she could not protect her kids from this potentially horrible battle. She mourned for all of the celebrations she would likely miss with them. She and Mike decided not to tell them when they first went to Dr. Thornton, but in December the decision was made with the confirmation. Patty knew that the diagnosis of ALS meant a slow progressive death sentence.

Patty educated herself on the typical progression and what to expect. Nerves that control muscle function reach from the brain and spinal cord to the muscles throughout the body. As these nerve cells degenerate or die, there is less innervation of the muscles and the person gradually becomes totally paralyzed. Speech is usually lost and the diaphragm is eventually affected, leading to an inability to breathe. Through all of this, the brain remains unaffected. Being immensely independent, Patty worried about loss of control and total dependence on others. She worried whether Mike could cope with being a caregiver. She was fearful about the dying process since she had watched her brother die, struggling for breath, from emphysema; another disease that affects the ability to breathe. Beyond all of these emotions was the question, "Why God?" We all asked that question.

How do we help someone else through devastating news, circumstances that we ourselves can't comprehend? Joan Chittister elaborates in *Scarred by Struggle, Transformed by Hope*: "Struggle is a very private thing. It happens in the very depths of our souls. Other people commiserate, of course, as they watch us struggle with the pain of losing, the meaning of endings, the shock of great change, the emptiness of the present. But they cannot really share our pain because what we have lost, however significant to us is not really significant to them. They advise but they cannot possibly know the cost of every step. It is not their arms that are heavy, not their legs that have gone to lead, not their 'knees that are weak' (Psalm 109). Those who stand at the edges of our life at such a time as this cannot realize the sense of deep, deep isolation that comes when life as we have known it has been suddenly extinguished."[6]

And so her friends listened as she poured out her gut wrenching fears, her questions to God, and her anger. What was God's plan? What were the lessons to be learned here? What did He want from her? Why did this have to happen to her? She wanted to see her children get married. She wanted to hold her grandbabies. She wanted to grow old with Mike, and she wanted to continue with her ordinary, mundane life! Would there be a miracle and would she be cured? Oh, how she prayed for this to happen. We hugged and cried a great deal during those days. She asked me questions as a professional, knowing that I had worked with paralyzed patients as a young nurse. My reactions were often those of a nurse; compassionate and yet courageously blocking the emotions that can so overwhelm those in the medical field who deal with disfigurement and death. In retrospect, this professional courage carried me through this journey despite the fact that it was occurring to one of my best friends.

Chapter 4

Two are better than one,
because they have a good return for their work;
if one falls down, his friend can help him up.
But pity the man who falls and has no one to help him up!

ECCLESIASTES 4:9, 10

Living nearby made me a perfect "'pick-me-up" person. I mean this literally, not figuratively. There were numerous times when Patty would fall at home and not be able to pull herself up alone. The stairs to their bedroom became extremely difficult and shortly after the diagnosis a stair glide was installed which certainly helped in conserving her energy. One Saturday morning when Mike was returning to town from business, she fell getting out of the bathtub. With the fear of falling had also come the reassurance of carrying the phone with her at all times. My husband, Neil, and I went to the house. After I got Patty partially clothed, Neil helped to lift her to a chair. It became more difficult to lift her alone since her ability to help was rapidly decreasing. She felt ashamed, and after Neil left she broke into tears. Another time she fell in the back yard and laid there until her neighbor saw her and helped her up. Despite the braces designed to help stabilize her ankles and the use of the cane, the falls still occurred. Sometimes it could happen simply when the dogs, Mulligan or Riley, brushed up against the back of her leg. Frustrated, I verbalized to K.C. that I felt they were a hazard and should be given up. Patty would never have considered it and I was to learn a valuable lesson down the road.

She was deathly afraid of falling as she knew that she could not effectively catch herself and fell quite hard at times. She would then have to call someone to help her, never knowing how many calls it would take before she could reach someone. The next stage was always the terrible humiliation of bothering people and relying on them. She often struggled on her own before resorting to making a phone call. I remember one morning when she had tried for an hour before reaching me. She was exhausted by that time and had very little strength left. I knew it was going to be impossible for me to help her alone yet she was determined that the two of us could succeed if only we could gradually move her to slightly higher surfaces. I went on a search and find mission throughout the house looking for anything that would bear her weight and gradually get her up to chair level. I remember being so annoyed and wanting to just give up since there was the risk of injury for both of us while trying! I finally became adamant, told her to forget it and went to find a neighbor to help. I couldn't find anyone available, so in frustration I called the Pittsford emergency squad who came and lifted her to the chair without any concern. But again, she felt as though she had inconvenienced them.

Patty also had several falls at work. Construction at the hospital's employee health site had forced the department to relocate into a temporary trailer. This introduced a confined space and more obstacles for Patty to maneuver around. On St. Patrick's Day 2004, while in a room with a patient she turned and fell backwards, striking her head on a scale used to weigh patients. She cut the back of her head requiring stitches in the emergency room. Scalp lacerations tend to bleed profusely as did this one and Patty was mortified that this occurred while she was working. Juanita had to seek assistance from the hospital to get Patty into a wheelchair so that she could be taken to the emergency room. This was a decisive turning point as Patty came to the realization that it wasn't safe for her to work.

Patty couldn't have Juanita taking care of her when they were so busy with patients. She also wanted to maintain control of this decision and not be told by her employer that she could no longer work. It was a difficult choice. She loved her job and was also aware that her paycheck was important in the financial plan to pay for the care she anticipated would eventually be needed. It felt like one more decline, and with it the deepening recognition of her inability to continue life as she had always known it. Basically it was another kick when she was down.

This was a painful decision, but the right one. Work was no longer safe for her or the patients. The forty-five minute drive each way to work was also a concern. Should she even be driving at this point? Fortunately that summer she did give up the keys. She also acquired a wheeled walker with a seat where she could sit and rest if needed during her outings. The walker was a lovely muted rose color and soon it was dubbed "Rosie."

It wasn't just the falls that were becoming an issue. As the muscles in her thighs weakened, Patty had trouble with basic functions such as getting up from the toilet. While she and Mike were visiting K.C. and Bill Legg in Florida in April, 2004, Mike was unable to help Patty up alone and so Bill had to assist. She felt so mortified that her dignity had been violated. My toilet experience with Patty is as vivid as yesterday. We had breakfast at Forest Hills and went to shop at a nearby grocery store. Patty needed to use the restroom, which turned out to be a single toilet facility. She went in alone and locked the door while I waited outside, and waited and waited and waited. A line was growing outside the bathroom waiting for it to become available. Finally she called out that she had been trying for five minutes but was unable to get up from the seat. This was quite the predicament, since the door was locked and I couldn't get to her! I went in search of a manager to get the key to unlock the door, apologizing to the other patrons as I left. After another five minutes I located the manager only to have him declare that he did not have the key and would "track it down." Another 5-10 minute wait ensued until I had the key in hand and could at last enter the restroom. Patty had finally pulled herself up, after struggling all of this time. She was so weak and tired that all we could do was leave and go home; however, I did take enough time to admonish the manager to have the key always available for emergencies. I never allowed her to go into a bathroom by herself again, let alone lock a door!

As May 2004 approached, so did the annual Women's retreat to Kentucky. Patty so desperately wanted to go since she had missed the previous year and knew in her heart that she would likely never go again. She asked everyone's opinion as though seeking affirmation. K.C. told her it was her decision. Mike did not want her to go since it would be a long distance to any medical care. Karen Nowlan, who led the retreat, was optimistic that she should go. From a medical and perhaps a selfish perspective, I was totally against it since I was unable to attend and help her. I felt Karen was unrealistic in encouraging her since she had never picked her up off the floor! Yes, Patty could do kitchen ministry since she could not do physical work; however, how was she going to get into the houses to do this? The uneven ground would surely cause her to fall even with Rosie, the rickety steps into houses would be impossible for her to climb and, ultimately, I was concerned that the trip would end up being about her needs not those of Booneville, leading to a misdirected experience for the other women attending.

I only voiced this latter concern to K.C., not Patty. Probably a large part of my negativism was due to my inability to give up control. Ultimately, she decided that she was going, although the night prior to leaving almost determined otherwise. Neil and I, along with Patty and Mike, went to the Legg's for dinner. While navigating the steps to leave, Patty suddenly fell backward with her head making a resounding thud on the foyer slate floor. It happened so quickly that none of us could begin to break her fall and we were aghast. She was not seriously hurt except for a terrific headache and her self-esteem, but Mike was even more adamant that she should not go. I can only imagine the conversations that night, but Patty was at the chapel the next morning; packed and ready for Kentucky with numerous "accessories": potty chair, lifters (made by Mike to gradually help her up from a fall), Rosie, and a wheel chair.

Allyson Bailey-Farchione was going on retreat for the

first time that year, and did not know anyone in the group. She first met Patty the previous Sunday at Mass when the group went forward for Fr. Mike Bausch to give them a special blessing. As she looked at Patty with her braces and walker she recalls thinking, "Oh, great, this is going to slow things down." Allyson did not know that one of the week's lessons would be learning to give up control. Her next meeting with Patty was in the bathroom at a rest area on the drive down. Patty needed help getting up from the toilet and Allyson was available. Allyson remembers, "The ice broke and layers of preconceived ideas peeled away when K.C. and I saw the leopard panties that Patty was wearing, a gift from her daughter. We were in hysterics." Despite the fact that Patty hated needing the help, a true friendship was born as well as fuel to tease her with in the coming years. During the week, Allyson said Patty opened up about her fears and the prospect of being helpless. K.C. shouldered the major care responsibilities for Patty such as giving her a shower, helping her get out of bed and get dressed and getting up in the middle of the night for bathroom calls. She had to have additional help for those. K.C. reminisces, "It was a wonderful trip for Patty (in spite of the restrictions on where she could and could not go). She met Louise for the first time and on Friday while everyone else was cleaning the Mission Center and getting ready to go home, we drove out to the 'holler' to see Louise and Millard for one more visit on the porch." In one week Patty forged a special bond with Louise that continued for the next two years.

K.C. had met Louise Rice on the Transfiguration retreat of 2003, the one Patty could not attend because of the fall in Boston. She returned home and told Patty about this wonderful woman she met named Louise. Louise was a mountain woman who had married at age thirteen, had her first child at fifteen, and was a grandmother at age 34. She had had a hard life in the mountains, suffered from depression after her husband passed away, and yet her determination and simple faith would be very powerful in Patty's journey.

Patty wrote, "*Louise has lived her whole life in the mountains . . . (K.C.) talked of how strong this incredible Louise was and how she had lived alone for several years after her husband Everett had passed away. She told the story of Millard coming to live on the mountain; his wife had died and he was returning to where he grew up. They soon became companions to each other. She went on to describe how far up in the holler Louise was; approximately four miles off the main road and you had to cross a tiny bridge over a creek to head up the mountain. Her home sits on five beautiful acres of mountain; there were birds, flowers and beautiful trees. K.C. said she found such peace walking and talking with Louise in her garden. She told me that Louise could sing and play the guitar and she had a very worn song hymnal that she used to sing from . . . I had never met Louise but I felt I was getting to know this incredible woman through another's eyes.*

In the fall of 2003 I developed some health problems and my dear friend K.C. was with me every step of the way; little did I know I had another angel walking with me in silence from far away. I can't remember exactly when it was but K.C. showed me an email she had received from Louise that said she was praying for me. She said she felt like she knew me even though we had never met and that she was sure I would be OK. She said she would continue to pray for me. In December, K.C. shared a cassette tape that Louise had recorded and sent to her in the mail. It was the most beautiful tape I had ever heard. She had many different songs on the tape; of course there was 'In the Garden', 'Whispering Hope', 'The Last Mile of the Way' and one of my very favorites, 'Silent Night.' To this day it still brings tears to my eyes when I hear her sing. It was a short time later that I began emailing Louise and sending her snail mail as well. We talked of many things in our notes to each other, and as the months passed I felt like I had known her my whole life.

In May of 2004 I finally was able to meet Louise in person for the very first time. What an incredible moment in my life! I had shared so much with her and here we were face-to-face and hugging each other; it is a feeling I cannot begin to describe. The next week was a week filled with so many beautiful moments shared with Louise and Millard. These moments will forever be remembered and treasured deep in my heart."

Patty wanted to do something special for Louise, and began an intensive project of printing Louise's life story, "My Memories of the Mountains." The above quotes about her life are taken from Patty's preface to that story. Louise sent Patty all of her writings and Patty translated them as best she could, and typed them into the computer. At times when she grew tired she had Greg and Aly type. By the time the project was completed, Patty could no longer type using her hands but was using a voice activated system on her computer. She then had multiple copies bound and printed. It truly was a labor of love.

Sr. Bea recalls, "How fondly I remember that last time she was in Kentucky, and how you all cared for her so well; what a struggle it was for her to get around, but she was determined. She said to me once, 'I feel like I'm not doing my share here' but I told her, Patty, you are doing more than any of us here through the witness of your life. How true it was, and how grateful she was to be there even amidst great odds and inconveniences. She was and continues to be a very precious person, and I am so grateful to God that I was privileged to have known her and all of you folks from Rochester. Yes, Booneville was privileged to have her touch their lives, as the folks there also touched her, especially Louise."

And so God knows better than Cindy, as Kentucky was exactly what Patty needed. She forged new friendships with Louise and the other Pittsford women, as well as meeting her need to see God a little more face to face. As a result of the bond these women had formed in Kentucky, they decided to start a prayer group in order to continue lending support to each other.

Chapter 5

For where two or three come together in my name,
there am I with them.

MATTHEW 18:20

M any concerns, needs, and petitions were brought
before the newly formed prayer group. Patty had a
major hurdle to surmount in June. As an early 26th wedding anniversary gift, the kids had given Mike and Patty a
trip to Hawaii. Although it was a trip of a lifetime, she had
real concerns about the logistics of traveling that far due to
her limited mobility. She tried to trust that details had been
completed and things would go well; yet intermittently she
considered cancelling. She knew there would never be another opportunity, she wanted the time with Mike and did
not want to disappoint the kids. K.C. had a major concern
about her inability to use an airplane bathroom. Before she
left on the trip, K.C. mentioned she might want to wear a
Depends to alleviate this concern. She might as well have
suggested that Patty hang a sign around her neck that said
INVALID. Patty made it quite clear that she was NOT going

to resort to that measure and there would be no further discussion! She and Mike did deal with some issues during the vacation and yet it also was a wonderful time for them. They were even able to rent a beach wheelchair that would go in the sand. This was the first experience Patty had with a motorized wheelchair.

Back in Pittsford it was becoming apparent to Patty's friends that she was going to need some help as she was no longer safe alone. K.C., Peggy and I often went to the house to help her get out of bed after she had a nap in the afternoon. K.C. and Peggy Brizee sat down and brainstormed possible resources for hired help as well as volunteers. K.C. suggested that perhaps some of the women from the Prayer group might be willing to assist. We felt that Peggy was the appropriate friend to have this discussion with Patty as she might be more accepting of her opinion. Interestingly enough, Patty and Mike had drawn the same conclusion and were looking for a private pay home health aide.

Insurance companies have regulations regarding coverage of home health aides for clients. Generally aide service can only be instituted if a client requires the services of a licensed nurse to assess and give care as well. Insurance coverage for both nursing and aide services have length of time limitations so these services are not available for long term chronic illnesses but reserved for acute health issues. Patty did not meet the insurance requirements since she had a chronic illness with no known end date and she also did not require any skilled nursing care; only help with daily care needs. Even if insurance would have covered aide service, Patty would not have had consistency in the aides sent by the agency which would have been difficult as the disease progressed.

Considering the out of pocket cost for private aide service, K.C. and I felt it would be vitally important if we could get a volunteer group together. The purpose would be to maintain her safety, help prepare her breakfast, do errands with the wheelchair and give her social interaction. If the volunteers could help in the mornings, then an aide would only be needed in the afternoon. As we began formulating this plan and asking for interest, Patty and Mike hired Aide #1 in August to come daily in the afternoon for four hours. Her responsibilities would be to fix lunch, help Patty to bed for an afternoon nap, help with exercises and do light housekeeping.

Patty's friends and family heard the call and ten volunteered to help in the mornings. Patty had to make the final decision as to who she felt comfortable with and who could be involved. In the best of times she had difficulty asking for help; in her vulnerable frame of mind it was a daunting experience. Greg reflects, "As you know and have said, my mom was extremely independent; she did not like asking for help and we all knew that. Throughout her final years here on earth I think we all learned that asking for help is okay." The plan was to arrive as Mike was leaving for work and stay until #1 arrived. It was decided that the group needed a name, FOP was suggested by Lynn but KC said she would rather be a FLOP instead of a FOP and the name stuck, Friends and Loved Ones of Patty Stachura. I was appointed the Major FLOP in order to plan a schedule for this varied group, taking into account days that they worked and had other commitments. One requirement was that they had to find their own replacement if unable to fulfill their obligation. We did not want Mike and Patty to worry about coverage and I was not going to get involved in what could potentially be a headache. Most people were scheduled every other week, except that K.C. had Wednesdays with Patty and I had Mondays with her.

Dave recalls what the formation of the FLOPS meant to him. "It was tough for me to be so far away (in Boston) and not be there to help like Aly and Greg could. It was also difficult to know what exactly was going on day to day with Mom's health. I talked to her and my Dad three-four times a week but both were focused, rightly so, on the positives rather than on the slow changes that were taking place. They obviously kept me up to date on things but I certainly did not know the little things that were happening. Hearing that the FLOPS had been organized was pretty powerful in many ways. It was great to know that so many people cared about her to put this together and be a part of it. It was also really nice to know that Mom would have people around her to spend time laughing and having fun. Seeing this group organized was a major wake up call for me as well. Although I knew what was ahead with ALS and knew some of the struggles Mom and Dad were going through, the formation of the group really hit home about how difficult this was going to become. Just knowing that Mom was in such good hands with all of the FLOPS was quite a blessing." Mike felt so much relief that Patty was no longer alone and he did not have to fret as much about her. Unfortunately everything was not going to run as smoothly as hoped.

Although Patty was glad to spend time with the FLOPS, she was not used to having someone around continuously. She told me she sometimes felt as though she had to entertain us. Also, this was one more step in giving up her autonomy and relying on others. As women, we were also accustomed to being decision makers and "doers"; thus, we had to learn to ask Patty how she would like to have things done and to let her make decisions. It was also difficult trying to train Aide #1 who had her own ideas about everything. When it came to household chores Patty wanted things completed "her way" and to "her standards". She had been in charge of her home and she just could not give up the management factor. In her mind, she could not control what was happening to her body, so she needed to control the extraneous circumstances around her. Aide #1's previous experience had mainly been with the elderly, so she was used to taking charge and making choices. She was unfamiliar with ALS and did not understand the progression of the disease; especially that, mentally, Patty was unchanged. She seemed to think that since her physical capabilities were diminished, it must be so for her mental capabilities; and with this way of thinking, she appeared to "talk down" to Patty. Reflecting on this, I think that a large part of the population believes this about the physically handicapped. Patty tried to give her information about her disease and the likely progression that would occur. Again, #1 did not seem to grasp the concept. She pushed Patty to do more for herself, to walk farther, to try harder and eventually Patty's body just could not do it; she would be exhausted. It was a very wearisome period.

Multiple decisions took place in the autumn of 2004. Kim Cawley, a respiratory therapist, suggested that Patty begin using Non-Invasive Ventilation (NIV) during naps and at night to help conserve her strength. The machine incorporates two separate pressures, one for inhaling and one for exhaling, to deliver a breath via a positive pressure mask that would be strapped to her face. Because of the two separate pressures of NIV, Patty would not need to use as much effort to breathe. Kim recalls, "Patty was very resistant to the idea. I really had to talk fast to sell her on it." Ultimately Kim was right, as it made her much more comfortable when she was lying flat.

Patty continued to be able to walk and use Rosie in the house. However when she went out she needed to use a wheelchair. She began having trouble transferring out of the Ford Explorer to use Rosie. She almost fell while transferring at church and realized the danger. Due to the increased risk of falling and her deteriorating mobility, the next step was to purchase a motorized wheelchair. The FLOPS took turns riding and steering it with the hand control, but no one caught on as quickly as Patty. Along with this decision came the next; to buy a handicapped van that would accommodate the wheelchair. Patty was like a kid in a candy store! She was so excited to get out of the house and go wherever she wanted to! Strapping her into the van was somewhat tricky, but we need not worry about forgetting any steps as she quickly filled us in. It was almost as though she would test me; as I was ready to back out she would calmly say, *"Do you think maybe you should buckle my seatbelt?"* Every day was go-out-to-breakfast-day now with these new wheels; and Forest Hills was doing a booming business on Wednesdays since the prayer group always met there after our prayer session.

Mike and Patty struggled with the decision of whether to stay in the house with her impending loss of mobility. They knew she would soon be totally reliant on the wheelchair and that would eliminate using the bedroom upstairs. They toyed with the idea of moving to a single level condo but Patty truly hated to leave the security of her known neighborhood. They knew they could make the dining room into a bedroom but that did not take into account remodeling a bathroom; Patty also did not want to consider this idea since it would constantly remind her of her inadequacies. They finally decided to build an addition behind the existing garage with a bedroom and handicapped bathroom. They found a builder who was familiar with handicapped situations as he himself had multiple sclerosis. The construction immediately put the house into a state of chaos.

As the Christmas season approached, it allowed the opportunity to extend some Christmas cheer by decorating Patty's wheelchair. She was a little unsure about this (rolled her eyes) as I arrived one Monday with tinsel for the wheels, Christmas angels to hang on the back and a flag that we attached saying Merry Christmas! Someone else bought battery operated twinkle lights and added those. We thought she looked quite jolly as we tooled around town Christmas shopping. She became more enthusiastic about this display when she saw the smiles around her and when strangers approached and told her how festive it was!

Patty was finally feeling comfortable with the FLOPS and looked forward to their visits each day. The interaction helped her keep a perspective on those around her rather than just focusing on the increasing loss she was experiencing. When Allyson was feeling particularly vulnerable one day, Patty empathetically shared with her that, *"sometimes what I'm going through doesn't seem so bad."* When the prayer group discussed a gospel relating to Jesus' healing power, she grew to comprehend that each of us has a need for some kind of healing in our lives. She became less self-absorbed, reached out and listened to our needs as well. While doing research for this book, I found Patty's undated prayer list in her computer which shows the love in her heart for those around her.

"This is my list that I want to pray for. It may be intentions for friends or things close to my heart.

- Prayers for my dad, that he not suffer and the Lord to take him peacefully.

- Please take care of Bev; her friendship and love have been so very important to me.

- For Mike, that in his work world things will become easier and more rewarding.

- For Dave, Alyson and Greg that their journey ahead will be blessed and guided by God.

- For each and every one of my FLOPS, they will never know how very deeply they have moved my soul, nourished my heart and helped deal with unthinkable changes in my life, without them and my family I would not be here.

- For Diane (her sister), she is always there for me no matter what.

- In thanksgiving for Margaret, Matthew and Natalie; they bring me such joy and happiness!

- For Brian and Eileen who are always there for me with love and support

- For Julie and Mike, the best niece and nephew I could have asked for.

- I pray for Connie that you keep her safe.

- Please keep Carolyn safe and able to handle the challenges ahead.

- Please pray for Sr. Bea, surround her with your love and protect her from pain.

- *Help Sr. Karen and her new work with the Hispanic people in Canton, Ohio*
- *Continue to hold Allyson close to you and guide her in this painful journey she is on."*

This growing awareness for the needs of others paralleled being asked to give a reflection at church during Advent services. In order to see the inner workings of God on her heart, here is Patty's reflection as written.

Chapter 6

Rejoice in the Lord always.
I will say it again: rejoice!
Let your gentleness be evident to all.
The Lord is near.
Do not be anxious about anything,
but in everything, by prayer and petition,
with thanksgiving, present your requests to God.
And the peace of God, which transcends
all understanding, will guard your hearts
and your minds in Christ Jesus.

PHILIPPIANS 4:4-7

"When I was asked if Mike and I wanted to do the (vesper) reflection for the third week of Advent my gut reaction was, no I don't think so . . . but I promised I would check with Mike first and we would talk about it. Well I guess you know what the answer was. I am not really good at speaking in front of a crowd because those who know me well know it is because I tend to cry very, very easily; so with that in mind please bear with me if I get a little teary.

When Gloria gave us the reading for tonight, I had many thoughts pass through my mind. Did you ever read a scripture passage and immediately feel as if it was written just for you? That is how I felt about this passage. It is very simple but contains a very strong message: Rejoice the Lord is near. Dismiss all anxiety from your minds. Present your needs to God, especially in petitions full of gratitude and you will find God's peace.

Rejoice and dismiss all anxiety from your mind. Not easy to do on a daily basis let alone during the Christmas season. As many of you know Mike, our three children David, Alyson and Gregory and I have had one heck of a year. After many months of symptoms and several more months of tests, I was diagnosed on December 17, 2003 with a form of ALS. ALS is also known as Lou Gehrig's disease. Well you want to talk about anxiety hitting you right between the eyeballs! This has been a year of many changes; too many to mention all of them, so I would like to share with you how some of these changes have impacted our lives and why tonight's reading is so powerful to me.

Anxiety has pretty much ruled my mind for a good year and a half now. Early on, I was filled with overwhelming anxiety and fear. I had many conversations with God; at first they were filled with prayers of hope and at the same time disbelief. Why was God doing this to me? Then they turned to anger, wondering how God could let this happen to me. Was I such a bad person? As the last year has unfolded, I have learned that our God is loving, kind and unbelievably patient. He works tiny miracles every single day; you just have to be open to see them. You have to be willing to trust in your faith and you have to be willing to give it all to God. I'm getting much better at this, but I still have days when I think God is not answering my prayers the way I want him to answer them so I try to take it all back on myself. I try to take back the control. God has a way of letting you know he's in control, but at the same time He gives you hope and courage and the strength to face the future.

You see, starting about a year ago, I put my needs in God's hands and pretty much told Him the miracle I needed. I'm pretty sure I didn't exactly practice that part about bringing my needs to him in petitions of gratitude. Over the last year, while I hoped for 'The big miracle' I have come to see the tiny miracles around me, and remind Him of how thankful I am for these gifts as well. Let me tell you about some of the tiny miracles. As I think about them, some of these miracles are not so tiny.

The first few months of the year, I did a lot of measuring of my capabilities. Was I getting worse or weaker? What would people think of me as my disabilities became more pronounced? Shouldn't I be able to accept this and stop crying about it? As I pray about it and think about where I am today, I am confident in the message of Corinthians that the Lord does not give us more than we can handle, and gives us a way out of our challenges so that we can endure them. Today I only measure what matters most in my life.

Last May I attended the women's trip to Kentucky. I was not sure I was going to go, right up until the night before we left. All of the women were my angels, making this trip possible. They gave me the gift of being able to minister to others in Kentucky. I still have a very deep attachment to Booneville and communicate with Sister Bea and Sister Karen often. I also correspond with a wonderful woman named Louise. She has been an inspiration and a tremendous source of encouragement for me. I draw strength from their example of simple and very deep faith.

In September a group of women in the parish organized sort of a formal team to help me every day with things I can no longer do for myself. Their example of unselfish giving is what St. Paul was talking about in the reading today.

Throughout the year several of the men of the parish have helped Mike and I with projects. One helped modify furniture so that I could use it. Another has given his time, during this very busy season, to help paint the handicapped accessible bedroom we are building.

It is nothing short of a miracle that we found a builder for the bedroom made up of a father and son team. The father, who is 72 years old, cared for his wife who had MS for over 30 years. She died in a car accident 18 months ago. The son has MS himself. They are truly sensitive to my physical needs, but more important is just how sensitive they are to the emotional side of things due to their first hand experience.

Many people have told us we are in their prayers, and have provided kind words and meals. It seems that these kindnesses come just when we need it most. As I think about it, I could tell you about little miracles for the next hour, but I think you see my point.

This Christmas, the Stachura family will continue to bring their needs to God, and continue to bring them in petitions of gratitude. As St. Paul taught, we have begun to feel God's peace in our lives, even though we do not always fully understand it.

Merry Christmas and remember, not only this season, but throughout the year, measure what matters in your lives."

Chapter 7

Consider it pure joy, my brothers,
whenever you face trials of many kinds, because you
know that the testing of your faith develops perseverance.
Perseverance must finish its work so that you may be
mature and complete, not lacking anything.
If any of you lacks wisdom, he should ask God,
who gives generously to all without finding fault,
and it will be given to him.

JAMES 1:2-5

P atty was beginning to find some peace with God and
the FLOPS were becoming indispensible. The interior of the bedroom addition was completed and Mike
and Patty moved downstairs. Patty and I had several dis-
cussions/debates about the purchase of a bed for the new
bedroom. She did not want to use twin beds as she did
not want to give up sleeping with Mike. At this point, she
could not turn herself and Mike would have to help turn
her during the night. She also knew she should get a special mattress to prevent pressure points since she was not
moving. Therefore she eventually came to the conclusion

that twin beds were needed but really struggled with this. I went a step further and suggested that she get a hospital bed which could be borrowed from the Muscular Dystrophy Association. This idea met with tremendous resistance. As painful as it was, I explained that she was eventually going to need it and economically it would be fruitless to buy a twin bed. I tried to make the idea more palatable by telling her she would be able to utilize the rails to help move herself around or turn a bit. She eventually followed my point of view and agreed to borrow the bed, another step on her journey and further giving of herself to God's control.

Patty continued to bring her requests to God at the prayer group. It had become apparent to Patty and Mike that Aide #1 did not have the appropriate personality for Patty's needs. Patty was indeed determined; however, Aide #1 made it very clear that she did not think Patty was trying hard enough to help herself. She also verbally criticized Greg one day for not doing more around the house. Patty was so livid that she would have thrown her out of the house that day if she had been capable. We began to see resentment building between them. As Aide #1's care spiraled downward, so did Patty's mood and she began searching for a replacement. Mike's friend, Bob Hutchins (Hutch), had a recommendation. Soon Aide #1 was dismissed and Aide #2 started. Patty was appropriately anxious about training someone new but she had confidence in Aide #2's skills and therefore also had more patience.

We were also having trouble lifting Patty from the toilet; it was nearly impossible for one person to do this and both Patty and the FLOPS were concerned about getting hurt. Patty began to do research into various lifts that

were on the market. A Hoyer lift was the first option but
Patty didn't like the bulkiness or the mechanics of how it
worked (having used them before on patients). She settled
on a Stella Stand Assist Lift which from then on was simply known as Stella. It consisted of various straps and a
hydraulic system that lifted her from sitting to a standing
position and then back down. This worked well because
it could be used for all of her needs: bed, shower chair,
toilet, and wheelchair. It was not simple technology! Since
Aide #2 used it more often she became very adept. But in-
variably, Patty would have to remind the FLOP- on- duty
about a forgotten step or exactly where to place her over
the toilet so that her "landing" was exact! She was fastidi-
ous about how you strapped her in and why wouldn't she
be? If something was forgotten, the straps would pinch
her or get wet on the toilet or she would be on the floor!
She truly had to put her trust in us; it is likely that she did
a lot of praying during those first few weeks of transfers!

In February 2005, our local paper, the Rochester
Democrat and Chronicle, asked for input from readers
as to what makes Pittsford special. Since Pittsford often
gets a bad reputation for being snooty, I wrote to them
on a whim about the FLOPS and the special friendship,
camaraderie and vocation that had emerged in this group
of Pittsford women. The editors were not only interested
in Patty and the FLOPS, but wanted to do a much larger
article on them. Having lost some of her self conscious-
ness, Patty was all for the idea, as long as it was about the
FLOPS and not just about her. She felt this would be a
tribute to us. Robin Flanigan was assigned as the writer
and brought Jay Capers with her as the photographer. The
article ended up being two full pages with photographs.

Patty had asked that they come on a Wednesday so that they could go to prayer group and breakfast with the group. They did a wonderful job of explaining ALS but also in portraying the importance of Patty's faith in God and her support through the FLOPS. Robin quoted Patty as saying, *"It's been hard for me because I was a very stubborn woman—well, I still am, but not as bad. I didn't want anybody's help. I didn't want anybody to know about this. You just figure you're going to handle this on your own, but you soon realize that it's bigger than you are."* After prayer, they followed us to Forest Hills for breakfast and were able to describe the help Patty needed with cutting her food, using her hand braces while eating, someone holding her cell phone for her to talk, and the banter that went back and forth. I explained to Robin, "Patty doesn't think she's doing anything for us, but our group has really become a community. We all have issues and we bounce them off

Cindy Tornes and Patty,
*Taken by Jay Capers and used with permission of the Rochester
Democrat and Chronicle*

each other. Patty's a big help with that. She opens up and makes it easier for us to open up as well."

They then went with her to the ALS clinic at Strong Memorial Hospital and watched during her exam with Dr. Charles Thornton. He shared that Patty's case was a little unusual in that her symptoms had progressed slower than most. Patty acknowledged that she felt the power of prayer had something to do with that. At the end of the article Robin writes, "Her faith has deepened since the diagnosis. In her bathroom, a passage from Corinthians is taped to the wall above the toilet-paper holder: 'God will not let you be tested beyond your strength. Along with the test God will give you a way out of it so that you may be able to endure it.' Patty has been using the passage for guidance since August 2003, the month she saw her first neurologist. She initially interpreted it to mean the doctors were going to be wrong about her diagnosis. Now she figures her way out is the disease's slow progression and the unimaginable support from family, friends and the FLOPS. And she endures." Robin quoted Patty, *"It's tough to be strong, but I think otherwise you don't have the hope,"* she says. *"You just hope that you get through every day. You try to look ahead—but not too far."*

The article was published in May and was met with much enthusiasm from the FLOPS as well as Patty. Robin brought the struggle of living with ALS and a small community of women to life in her story. We felt that readers were not only educated about the disease but we hoped that readers would also see Pittsford women in a new light, one of strength, prayer, consideration and sensitivity. Several months later Patty shared that she had been keeping contact with Robin through email. She said Robin had revealed that the opening song played on that Wednesday at Prayer was especially touching to a situation in her own life. It was a song about trusting in God rather than relying on your own concept of things. I found it so relevant that God was reaching out to not only Patty and the FLOPS, but to other people who came into contact with her.

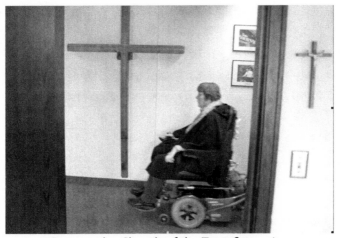

Patty at the Church of the Transfiguration
Taken by Jay Capers and used with permission of the Rochester Democrat and Chronicle

It is difficult to comprehend the complexity of feelings that Patty had. She felt grateful for God's graces and the friendship, laughter, camaraderie and support of the FLOPS and her family. Although she was over the bitterness; fear, sadness, and depression still raised its head. In less than two years she had seen herself go from a vibrant, independent, career woman to one who needed to use a wheelchair, hand braces, special eating utensils, and a NIV machine to breathe at night. She had to have someone help her with all of her personal needs such as showering, brushing her teeth, combing her hair and toileting. One can only imagine the emotions she endured.

Chapter 8

*For I am the Lord your God, who takes hold of your right
hand and says to you, Do not fear; I will help you.*

ISAIAH 41:13

Imagine:

- That your nose or head itched and you couldn't scratch it.
- Lying in your backyard unable to get up and not knowing
  when a neighbor might come home or hear you calling.
- That you had something in your eye and couldn't remove it.
- That your toe was bent down in your shoe but you couldn't
  fix it.
- Someone else had to brush your teeth for you every day.
- That you were taking a pill and it got caught in your throat.
- You were so sad that you were crying profusely and couldn't
  wipe your eyes or nose.
- You wanted to read a book but couldn't turn the page.
- There was a tight strap around your chest and you couldn't
  breathe deeply.
- That strap was pinching your skin and you couldn't move it.
- Being lifted by straps and totally relying on someone else to
  keep you from falling.
- That the brush of anything against the back of your knees

would cause you to fall and there was no way of catching yourself.

- Someone telling you to "just try harder" when you couldn't move your legs because you were so tired and weak.
- Being unable to wipe your mouth when you eat.
- Having someone feed you in a restaurant.
- Having diarrhea but it takes 8-10 minutes to get you on the toilet.
- Someone tying your shoes and not knowing how tight to make them.
- Someone tending to your hemorrhoids.
- Not being able to hug your loved ones.
- Not being able to cough and clear your throat.
- Relying on someone else to comb and style your hair everyday.
- Lying on your arm and it goes numb but you can't move.
- Not being able to take a deep breath.
- Lying in bed and your clothes are wrinkled under you.
- You can't floss your teeth if you have food caught.
- Being so angry at someone but you can't tell them because you rely on them to care for you.
- Letting someone else take care of your personal hygiene when you go to the bathroom.
- Having to go through an alley and the kitchen door in order to get into a restaurant.
- Not being able to be intimate with your spouse because it makes it difficult for you to breathe and you panic.
- Instead of a lover, your spouse must be a caregiver.
- Knowing you can't cough and worrying about choking.
- Not being able to put on your own deodorant let alone shave your own legs or armpits.
- Your underwear being twisted and you can't fix it.

- A mosquito flying around you and you can't swat it.
- You arrive at a funeral and are told by the representative, "Don't go over there (where your friends are sitting), you won't fit and I don't want you to dent the walls. Just stay right here (in the doorway), and watch out for my woodwork."
- Having that same person try to push your motorized wheel chair causing you to slightly fall forward, knowing that you are unable to catch yourself.
- Being unable to get out of your handicapped van in your wheelchair unless you have a handicapped parking space and someone has unlawfully parked there.
- Your hip intensely hurting and not being able to wake your spouse (since he gets 4 hours of sleep/night) to turn you.
- Having someone hold a conversation about you as though you weren't even in the room.
- Having to repeat yourself over and over because people can't understand what you are saying.
- Knowing that you are putting a financial burden on your family and that insurance does not cover many of your needs because ALS is a chronic not acute disease.
- Knowing that you likely will never see your children get married or have grandchildren.
- Going to support meetings and a person you had shared with two weeks ago has died.

Once we comprehend these things, we come to understand Patty's (and many other's) struggles with this terrible disease.

Chapter 9

For he will command his angels concerning you to guard
you in all your ways; they will lift you up in their hands
so that you will not strike your foot against a stone.

PSALM 91:11, 12

From the time she awoke until she would lie down at night, each day was a battle for Patty. The physical strain had a routine to it, but she wrestled with new emotions elicited by even the smallest happenings as well as with the ongoing spiritual free-for-all occurring inside her. She had come through Elisabeth Kübler-Ross' stages of grief: denial, anger, bargaining, and was sandwiched between the depression and acceptance phase.[8]

In the spring of 2005, Neil and I were making a seven hour drive to Ohio to visit family. Since we are country/ western music fans, the radio was tuned to a local station. Tim McGraw's song, "Live Like You Were Dying," came on. As I listened to the lyrics, tears began streaming down my face and I turned to Neil and choked, "That's exactly what Patty is doing in real life."

She wanted to pack in as much as she could each day. She had always enjoyed going out to eat and having good food; now she relished those meals even more since she knew she would not always have the ability to swallow them. She and Aly talked daily on the phone and Dave and Ericka made many more trips back from Boston than they normally would have. While she was still mobile, she went to visit her Dad who was in a nursing home in Buffalo. She enjoyed the company of her young niece, nephew and great niece who were perfectly comfortable with her equipment and the digression of her voice when that occurred. She went shopping and to the movies. Alan, her hairdresser, came to her house to fix her hair which always lifted her mood; she had body massages at home to help with her painful joints. All of these things gave her so much pleasure and yet she could not stop the progression of ALS nor ever push it from her mind.

As a diabetes educator, I often speak about my daughter's diagnosis of Type 1 diabetes. The hardest part of the disease was never having a break from it nor ever "putting it on the back burner"; it is a 24/7 disease. As she was growing up, her care, her health was always in the forefront of my thoughts. How much simpler that now seems since I know the final outcome of our labor, unlike Patty's, will be stronger health not death.

Some of the FLOPS use "The Word Among Us: Daily Meditation Guide" and I am often touched with reflections that apply to struggles in our lives as well as how our lives touch others. The meditation for September 26, 2008 is one of those.

"Ironically, the key to weathering the storms of life is often found within those very difficulties!

For those of us who already know the Lord, these are times when we can reach out to him and deepen our faith. For those who are still searching for God, hardship can be the doorway that opens their hearts to his mercy and grace. But there's another reason why some difficulties are blessings in disguise. God doesn't bring us through them merely for our own benefit, but for others as well.

God gives us his strength so that 'we may be able to encourage those who are in any affliction' with the same strength we have received from him (2 Corinthians 1:4). When we are going through a painful experience we may not realize how much it will benefit someone else later—not the pain itself, of course, but sharing how God helped us deal with it!"[9]

It wasn't until Holy Week of 2008 that I had this sudden revelation about the Passion of Christ. Patty's grapple with her inevitable death was much like Christ's! Christ was fearful; he did not want to be crucified. Jesus went with his disciples to Gethsemane; "He took Peter and the two sons of Zebedee along with him, and he began to be sorrowful and troubled. Then he said to them, 'My soul is overwhelmed with sorrow to the point of death. Stay here and keep watch with me.' (Matthew 26:37-38)" He prayed, much like Patty did, "… My Father, if it is possible, may this cup be taken from me. Yet not as I will, but as you will." (Matthew 26:39).

And yet Patty's struggle didn't beat her down, it changed her. Joan Chittister affirms this thinking, "When life changes under our feet, despite our resistance, without our permission, it is an invitation to growth. Change is an invitation to see life differently now than I did before."[10] Consequently, crises may actually be a motivator for conversion and redirection.

Patty became more reflective, not only concerning her own circumstances but about those around her as well. She visited Connie's husband, Bill Wahl, who had myotonic muscular dystrophy. After Patty left, Bill said, "We spoke about the fact that we aren't afraid of death, but the suffering beforehand." She kept in close contact with Louise and Millard. She took a genuine interest in friends she met at the ALS meetings, sending emails and remembering them at our prayer group. She became a voice for the disabled. The wind blew in powerful directions when she found a car parked in a handicapped space without the appropriate tags. On several occasions K.C. or I was forced to write a formidable note with colorful language strategically placed on a windshield. She once reported a car to an officer driving by the parking lot.

Peggy recalls another episode the first summer that the new library in Pittsford was open. "She wanted to rip the building supervisor a 'new one' because the handicapped access button on the rear of that giant library was too high and there was no button inside the double doors for entrance to the main lobby. (I think she did write the Pittsford Town Supervisor a letter about that.) In yet other instances Patty pointed out the problems of accessibility. As I am sure happened with other FLOPS as well, she acutely sensitized me to the issues of accessibility, which has had a lasting effect on me." I too became more aware of the needs of the disabled as noted by my detailing the problems with the design of handicapped bathrooms to my daughter who was studying Interior Design.

As the women of Transfiguration went to Booneville that May, Patty was sad to be left behind. However, it did not dampen her enthusiasm for the women who could go; nor her sense of humor. Patty had been placed in the position of Mother Superior the previous year in Booneville. This "honor" is bestowed by the retreat leader on someone she feels needs some encouragement and growth and is responsible for leading morning and evening prayers. Patty sent the following letter to K.C. to be read on arrival.

April 29, 2005

"My dearest friend KC,

You are so very special to me. I wish you a week filled with peace, tranquility, prayer, PATIENCE and many, many blessings. You know I wish I could be with you more than anything, but God must have some work here for me to do instead….Please give my friends a hug and kiss from me and tell them I keep them in my prayers and of course you know to give Louise (& Millard) the biggest hug of all. She has been an angel by my side and has lifted me so many times…..she will never know.

Remember I am with you in spirit. I will pray for all of you every day. Think of me when you wake up in the middle of the night. That's when you'll be really glad I'm not there physically…..hahahahahaha.

Okay a few words from Mother Superior (I am still the reigning Mother Superior until a new one is appointed. Isn't that Papal Law?)

• *For (the newbies) Lois and Nancy, enjoy the experience,*

leave behind all expectations, go with the flow and you will experience a peaceful and joyful week like no other. But if all else fails find KC. She has her satchel and she can pull most anything out of that satchel.

- Karen, stick to your plan. I know you have one even if you misplaced it. Seriously, you have a gift, a wonderful gift of being able to minister to the spiritual needs of women. (But you know if you get stuck Mother Superior is just a phone call away....hahahaha).

- Jennifer, I know you will have a very special week and you will be in my prayers. However, I do have one suggestion. I don't think you should take any 'four wheeler' rides with Millard. Trouble always seems to find you two.

- Connie, my dear Connie, I wish I could be there with you. You always make me laugh. You bring so much joy to all those you touch. Be patient and remember to look for God every day for He is in the tiny miracles of each day.

- Sister Bea, I will miss seeing you this year. You know you hold a very special place in my heart. Take a ride up the ski lift for me. Remember how scared I was to ride that thing?

- Sister Marge, though we have never met, I feel like I have gotten to know you through the eyes of Louise. Hopefully we will meet one of these days.

Well, I guess that is all from the reigning Mother Superior and remember there is nothing that duct tape can't fix! Have a blessed week! Love you,"

Patty

Patty was no longer self conscious about her appearance

or about trying to fit in to the Pittsford style of living. This was so aptly articulated by Frank Krause, who also had ALS and wrote the devotional, *My Dad's Love*. "When you know you haven't got long to live, the fear of man is gone, because you have nothing to prove."[11] She had shifted beyond those concerns since she knew that she was loved and accepted by a whole group of Pittsford women who came to spend time with her each day. Patty, who had once closed off her emotions to others, now released a fountain of revelations; and these in turn opened the hearts of those around her.

Patty and K.C. Legg

Chapter 10

*By this all men will know that you are my disciples,
if you love one another.*

JOHN 13:35

Patty felt truly blessed to have so many wonderful friendships in the FLOPS. Over and over she would tell us
that she did not know what she would do without us. This
part is true, because even though we did not know what she
truly was going through, we indeed filled many needs in
her life. One of those was just to listen....

We listened to her complain: about Aide #2, about each
other, about her kids (mostly as to why they weren't getting
married), about her disease, and about Mike. If something
isn't done correctly, who do we usually get the angriest at?
The person we love the most of course, because we feel the
most secure with them. Often, poor Mike got it with both
barrels! The biggest problem occurred if he forgot to consult
with her about something. That could range from a decision about the Aide to a comment made while on the telephone. Patty wanted the final decision on everything and
her famous comment was that even though she could not

do anything else she could still use her brain! I remember arriving on some Monday mornings to hear her muttering about not being able to wake Mike to turn her during the night... *"and I lay there three hours with him snoring away!"* Mike would just smile, give her a kiss, and say "yes, dear" as he left for work. The FLOPS affectionately dubbed him, St. Mike. We knew that not only was Patty's illness a toll on him emotionally but also physically. Mike had made arrangements regarding his work hours in order to be flexible for the FLOPS arrival in the mornings and when the Aide needed to leave at night. After putting Patty to bed, he would often stay up to complete work on his computer that he had not finished, many times going to bed at midnight. He then was up every hour or two in order to turn and reposition her; sometimes also taking her to the bathroom which would require an additional 20-30 minutes. He once shared with me that he averaged 4 hours sleep per night during the last 2 years of Patty's illness. K.C. recently forwarded a reading she had received over the internet which is posted on many websites without information on authorship. It is called, *"Is, Has Been, Will Be, Will Not Be!"* She said it reminded her of Patty and Mike with its concluding remarks:

"True love is neither physical, nor romantic.
True love is an acceptance of all that is, has been, will be, and will not be. The happiest people don't necessarily have the best of everything; they just make the best of everything they have."

Author Unknown

We listened to her concerns but this was also reciprocated, since we shared what was happening in our own lives, she would often express her worry for each of us.

Perhaps one of our children didn't have a job, or we didn't like the moral decisions they were making. Several of us experienced some serious health problems during our time with her as well as spiritual and emotional unrest. She also had many fears as to how Mike was coping. She knew that he was apprehensive about his job and therefore worried about everything from their finances, to his health, to his ability to continue caring for her. Some evenings, at her suggestion, I would sit with her so that Mike could go out for coffee with my husband Neil or some of his other friends from Men's Fellowship at Transfiguration. Patty fully knew that Mike's unwavering faith and love would be what carried him through this journey.

We listened to her ramble. Patty was never short of conversation; perhaps because she knew that one day she would not be able to speak. She told us about her conversations with her dad, her sister Diane and her friend Juanita that she had worked with. She kept us updated on her daughter Alyson's second grade students at school. I even took her to meet them once when they were on a field trip at a local park. Aly introduced her mom and they were fascinated with her motorized wheelchair and the lift on the van. Aly shared, "She was thrilled to meet them and they were excited to be introduced to her. I think it meant a lot for them to see how 'cool' her wheelchair was and she was happy for them to be able to experience someone in a wheel chair and realize she was no different. I could tell she was exhausted that day but very determined to make it out there to see my kids. Apparently she made a HUGE impression on one of the students, Nicole Wright, who has participated in and raised money for the ALS walk every year since." Nicole's mother, Linda, shared that Nicole was recognized in 2008 by the Upstate NY Chapter of the ALS Association for her fundraising achievements at such a young age; obviously another young life that was touched by meeting Patty.

Patty informed us that Greg was dating Aly's roommate, Sara Beth, and how she was hopeful that Greg would find the right girl to share his life with. She kept us posted on Dave and Ericka's life in Boston. We heard about her sister-in-law's struggle with a brain tumor and her concern for her. She chatted about the neighborhood gossip and we heard the latest news on Louise and Millard, Sr. Bea and Sr. Karen in Booneville.

We listened to her laugh as well as to the laughter she elicited from us. Days with Patty were not full of doom and gloom and talk of death. Much of the time our hearts were light, as though God was lifting them a bit.

- Bev tells about the phone call she received one morning from Patty after evidently passing her on the road somewhere in Pittsford. She called to say, *"I just saw Louie (Bev's dog) driving down the road in your car!"* Bev is short and with Louie on her lap, Patty couldn't even see her!

- Becky had many tales of driving, near misses and accidents to keep Patty amused (unless she happened to be driving Patty in her van that day!)

- I would sometimes call her in the evening and ask, "Want to go for a walk?" just like in the old days. She would crank her wheelchair up to Level 4 and laugh as I breathlessly tried to keep up.

- Whenever Connie came to visit and no matter what the conversation, there was laughter; and Patty laughed for days after.

L to R: Back: Peggy, Lynn, Sue, Allyson, Cindy, K.C., Karen
Front: Jennifer, Patty, Bev, Denise

- She enjoyed trying to pit the FLOPS against each other as she rated who made the worst/best coffee (Lynn's was chewable). Major fun at our expense!

- During Wednesday Prayers, if she was ready to go to breakfast, she and Lynn would catch each other's eye while the other pious prayers' eyes were usually closed. She'd then mouth to Lynn, *"AMEN"* so that Lynn would say it aloud and she could go eat!

- One day Lynn opened the van ramp onto a Lexus that was illegally parked in a handicapped spot and the lady was walking toward it when the ramp started coming out. Luckily it only hit the tire, although Patty wouldn't have cared!

- Patty always laughed when visiting my 83-year-old mother, because she was sassy and would still put her 50+ daughter *"in her place."*

To be a powerful listener.... what a mighty attribute for us to strive for. Bertie Shrader writes in *"Stranger in the House"*, "Everyone has a story to tell. And one of life's greatest joys is the privilege of listening."[12] What is more therapeutic than being listened to? After all, when we pray aren't we hopeful that God is listening? Is that not why we are told to "throw all your cares on Him"? Our spirits are often healed by revealing ourselves in prayer. And yet, how often do we take note of God's words of wisdom to us? I think that through listening to Patty, we were listening to God, to his calling, and to his loving invitation to do His will.

Chapter 11

Cast your cares on the Lord and he will sustain you;
he will never let the righteous fall.

PSALM 55:22

Things had gone pretty well throughout the spring of 2005, Patty remained fairly stable and in pretty good spirits. She found joy in living in the moment as seen one evening when she called and insisted that Neil and I come to the house to see her evening primrose blooming. She was so excited to share it with us as we sat outside on a beautiful evening talking and laughing while Neil teased her endlessly about being so keyed up over a plant.

In May, the family traveled to Boston for Greg's graduation. I remember them loading all of the equipment in the van including Stella, which was no easy feat. Mike writes,

> "She was very anxious about the trip but determined to go. We stayed at a hotel near the Charles River where we always stayed. Normal was very good. We had the only handicap accessible room which meant the bed was a bit higher and the bathroom

had minor modifications. Logistics were not easy. We stayed two or maybe three nights. Many times when we were alone on the trip she told me how proud she was of all the kids. I remember graduation having some sort of weather issues; I think it was unseasonably cold and rainy. It was very uncomfortable for her but she made the best of it. During this trip Dave had to help with some bathroom stops which she took in stride and later told me how much she appreciated him helping without hesitation.

Driving to graduation I ran over a curb and cracked a side rocker panel on the van. I never lived it down; but I earned it. I believe Dave had moved from South Street to a better part of town. She was not able to see his apartment as it was on the second floor. She did not make a big deal of it, but it was a big deal to her. She cried about it when we were alone. We took a short walk on the trail along the Charles River and talked about all of the runners and rowers. She missed being able to exercise, but was grateful to have made the trip. She insisted that I take a half hour run on the river first thing in the morning while she stayed in bed. She knew I needed the energy release and of course she was right. The drive both ways was filled with music from her many CDs, especially play lists from Aly and the FLOPS. Not a lot of talking; a lot of thinking/reflecting. No potty breaks on the drive, so we needed to make the trip on one tank of gas. It was a close call each way.

On the way to Boston Patty commented that this

was likely the last time she would be in Boston. I told her I thought that she was doing great and that we would do it again. We both knew better. It was one of the more difficult moments for both of us. On the way home we had three vehicles traveling together Aly in the Pathfinder, Greg in the Explorer, and us in the van. We talked on the walkie talkies and cell phone and had a grand time."

This was a period of change for Greg which ultimately made Patty quite happy. He explains, "It was tough for me to find a job in Boston, and I think the Lord had a hand in that. It forced me to come home, which not only led to the wonderful job I now have, but allowed me to live at home upstairs. I was able to come home after work and get some great meals from the FLOPS and, more importantly, spend time with my mom; especially towards the end."

Peggy talks about the trips that the two of them made to Canandaigua to see Juanita, the nurse she had worked with previously. "I would go to Devonwood Lane never quite knowing what Patty had in store for me! She'd announce that we'd be going to see Juanita and off we'd go. This endeavor was a strenuous undertaking, both physically and emotionally, for Patty; but she really looked forward to it. The drive to and from Canandaigua was always eventful, with task-master Patty instructing me as to how to drive the van and where to go! (She was always telling me where to go!)"

Peggy continues, "Patty looked forward to seeing Juanita and her other former co-workers. These visits were always very poignant; and the personal and professional bonds between Patty and Juanita were obviously very strong. An hour or so later I'd pick Patty up and, after tearful 'good-byes', we'd return to Devonwood Lane." Juanita explained, "I knew Patty in a different way than most of her friends. I ran the Employee Health Office by myself at Thompson Health. The job responsibilities kept growing and finally it was decided that I needed a part time nurse. One of the best decisions that I have ever made was to hire Patty. She was very bright, industrious and quite knowledgeable in office management. She also was very strong willed and firm in her convictions. No challenge was too great for her and she was my best supporter. We liked each other and supported each other almost instantly. We made a great team. We didn't even have to talk to each other to know just what to do. We were so in sync that Patty would start something and I would just pick up and complete it or vice versa. She was very moral and I trusted her completely. We worked together well, but my greatest blessing was that we also became friends. Even though I had not met her children, I knew all about them and how proud she was of them."

Mike recalled, "We had many wonderful visits with friends. She very much enjoyed visiting friends at their homes. It made her feel 'normal' to be invited into someone's home. There were always lots of laughs and very good times. The retractable ramp got a lot of use and after some engineering we built the threshold step and mini ramp. This combination of tools allowed her entry into all the homes to which we were invited. I recall numerous visits to the Legg's, Tornes', Farchione's, Klotz's, her brother Brian's, and niece Julie. There were a few ramp issues with spinning tires or the ramp unloading onto wet grass. I believe we may have left ruts in several lawns, and tire tracks in several homes which she always commented on during the drive home. These trips were enormous gifts for her and very uplifting. The party at Julie and Mike's for Natalie's first birthday (Patty's great niece) was memorable for several reasons: lots of kids. She loved kids and was thrilled that they were not afraid of the wheelchair and that they loved her just as Aunt Patty. Kids energized her. Opportunities to gather with family were always wonderful. Julie's friends all called her Aunt Patty (after staying at the Stachura's for Julie and Mike's wedding) and treated her as Aunt Patty, which was very special to her as well."

"In the fall," Mike explained, "Aly brought some of her teacher friends to our house for dinner and we had the introduction to Sara Beth. I believe the first date for Greg and SB was Dec 23, 2005. That was another huge event for Patty. From the beginning she just knew that SB was a keeper, something we all knew by the spring. I think I can say this was when she stopped worrying about whether her baby would be okay. It provided a calm for her in an important place in her heart." Aly recalls this event as well, "Yes, didn't we all know that she was something special. I remember dad saying how amazing she is to come into a situation like this and be the way she is. She was SO helpful with everything and fit right into our family from day one. I remember that night driving home in the car talking to SB about Greg, and thinking, hmmmm, could this really happen? I also remember Greg saying to me just a few weeks before this, 'You guys are so lucky that mom will at least always know your future husband and wife.... she'll probably never get to meet mine.' Then along came SB!!! Somebody's always looking out for us!"

Diane told me about visits Patty made to see her father in an Assisted Living facility in Buffalo: "Those I definitely remember. Patty would always bring a full lunch for Dad even if he had just eaten, and of course he would polish it off with no problem. He always enjoyed seeing Patty so much and if he couldn't come up with her name, he would call her 'the Rochester one'.... The trips to see Dad were extremely fun, but the end of the trip was nerve wracking because it had been hours since she had gone to the bathroom and she was thirsty but limited her intake. It was a mad dash into the house and bathroom for sure."

"There was also an ambulance trip to the hospital when she almost passed out while in the bathroom with Aide #2," Mike remembers. "That was a very difficult time. It tested her patience. It's bad enough to have the ambulance arrive to take care of you, but to find you on the toilet is a bit humiliating, especially when you know the ambulance driver! While racing home, I was able to put the paramedic in contact with Dr. Thornton who cleared the way for Patty at the emergency department. The visit to the ED at the hospital was a traumatic experience she was determined not to repeat. I believe she started to think about what was coming; it helped her decide what treatments to refuse."

Although there was no dramatic progression of Patty's ALS during this period, K.C. and I raised the question of what Patty wanted as far as emergency measures. Patty was not ready to make a decision about end of life issues yet. We felt that she should have something in place and reinforced that it could always be changed but it was not really our place to force the issue. Patty did come across a document called "Five Wishes" which she felt expressed her needs more than a Living Will; however, she wasn't prepared to fill it out just yet.

Patty's experience with Aide #2 in general had been

good. As Robin had mentioned in the newspaper article, they bantered back and forth like two old married folks. Patty had planted three kinds of basil in the garden and Mike recalls that the two of them made pesto sauce at least two-three times a week. Patty was proud to share this with special people. Mike feels that Patty "taught her a lot about taking care of a home and garden. Patty walked her through some issues with contractors and a grant from the city to rehab her own home." Patty was confident in the care she was given and felt that Aide #2 listened to her and treated her *"like she had a brain."* Mike explains, "She trusted her as a friend, not just as a caregiver." Thus it was difficult for Patty to give any negative feedback to her even when it might be needed. Things started to change in late summer when Aide #2's mother died and she needed to travel to NYC on weekends and often would take an extra day along with it. Her daughter lived there as well and had some problems she needed help with. This proved difficult for me as I then needed to find added FLOPS coverage to be with Patty. Most of us were willing, but with some of us working, with appointments and other commitments, it was not easy to add extra days to our schedules. As Thanksgiving approached, Aide #2 said she needed to be gone for a few weeks and had found a friend who was also an aide to cover for her. This sounds generous but in reality it was a major upheaval for Patty.

Patty's routine was very regimented which gave her a certain amount of reassurance. She would need to teach a new aide her entire schedule and became quite anxious about this. Explanations were also harder since her speech was a bit more difficult to understand. Routine tasks involved using Stella to get her out of bed, onto the toilet, into the shower chair and the wheelchair; and obviously it was imperative that this was all done correctly and safely. Patty needed to be put to bed in the afternoon for her nap and her NIV machine needed to be regulated; and in order to be comfortable in bed she especially needed to be positioned precisely. Her wheelchair had to be anchored into the van whenever errands needed to be run. This didn't even take into account the basic personal care of showering, brushing her teeth and feeding her that was required. Once again, Patty became depressed.

Aide #3 was very nice and learned very quickly. As a "couple of weeks" soon became a month, Patty found that she was adjusting to Aide #3. She was easy for Patty to talk to and in fact, Patty began to think she was more reliable and appropriate for her needs than Aide #2. Patty, however, was reluctant to contact Aide #2 to get a definitive return date even though most of the FLOPS continuously prompted – a nice word for "insisted" by K.C. and myself – her to do so. Having been close to her, Patty did not want to cause a big scene even though she was now faced with the possibility that she would not return at all. Aide #3 had another job pending in January and could not continue long term. Finally, Mike and Patty agreed that Aide #2 either had to return or be terminated. If she was not coming back to work, they needed time to secure someone new and train her. Aide #2 did return in early January but there was an obvious attitude change in her. She no longer seemed to have as much patience with Patty. Patty, on the other hand, had also lost some trust and confidence in the aide. It was a tense period of time. Patty finally blew up one day and told her not to return even though she was clueless as to what the next step would be. She only knew that she could not become as personally involved with the next caregiver.

Chapter 12

He said to his disciples, "Why are you so afraid?
Do you still have no faith?"

MARK 4:40

A s things deteriorated with Aide #2, Wednesday prayer group and breakfast was not only a venting board for Patty but a constant means of support during this upheaval. Even so, in January a thread of discord became recognizable during the discussion of the Gospel reading from Mark 4:35-41:

That day when evening came, he said to his disciples, "Let us go over to the other side."
Leaving the crowd behind, they took him along just as he was, in the boat. There were also other boats with him.
A furious squall came up, and the waves broke over the boat, So that it was nearly swamped.
Jesus was in the stern, sleeping on a cushion.
The disciples woke him and said to him,
"Teacher, don't you care if we drown?"

He got up, rebuked the wind
and said to the waves, "Quiet! Be still!"
Then the wind died down and it was completely calm.
He said to his disciples, "Why are you so afraid?
Do you still have no faith?"
They were terrified and asked each other,
"Who is this? Even the wind and the waves obey him!"

Along with this reading was the following meditation taken from "The Word Among Us," January 2006:

Teacher, don't you care? (Mark 4:38)

These words, shouted by the disciples over the roar of the storm, could easily be our own. The wind was howling, the boat was filling with water, and it was hard to remember that Jesus was there. Desperately doing all they could to stay afloat, the disciples finally called out in exasperation for Jesus, feeling abandoned and despondent.

How many times does the same thing happen to us? Our lives may be sailing along happily and we feel that we are in the Lord's hands. Then a storm suddenly arises. A loved one dies. We are diagnosed with a life-threatening illness. A child gets into serious trouble. Our marriage seems on the rocks. Each of us knows what it would take to "rock our boat." For a while, we may be able to keep afloat, but sooner or later, we cry out in despair, "Lord, don't you care?"

When we are in the midst of it, we are naturally overwhelmed by the immediacy of the storm confronting us. Like the disciples, we may forget that Jesus is still with us in the boat. We feel abandoned by God; we may even think he is out to get us because he brought us into the storm. If he really loved us, why would he be asleep, oblivious to our desperation?

But the truth is that Jesus is never unaware of what we're going through. He is always with us and always cares deeply for us. Just because he's in the boat, however, doesn't mean we won't come up against any storms. When we cry out to him, we can see that he is closer to us in the storms than at any other time. He may or may not calm the storms but he will always speak peace to our hearts.

The next time you face the storms of life, do your best to look beyond the waves and the wind. Look at Jesus, who has always been sitting right next to you, and trust him to steer you through to your destination.

Lord Jesus, sometimes I just can't rise above the storms I face in my life. The trials seem so hard, and it feels as if you are far from me. Help me to look up and see you looking at me with love. Raise me up so I can keep my eyes on you! [13]

Naturally, as the group began discussing the text we thought of Patty's situation. Nevertheless, many of us described events in our own lives where we felt Jesus seemed very far away from us while asleep in our boats, so to speak. Patty piped up, *"I think he's damned comatose in mine!"* Dead silence! We were a bit aghast even though most of us were accustomed to her frankness. I think the underlying current was that we understood why she would say that; all except K.C. and she was mortified. Long after the group had departed she discussed the exchange with Patty. K.C.

had serious concerns as to whether Patty was a true believer as she ventured off to Florida in February and March. Conversations flew back and forth via email for weeks between the three of us as well as discussion continuing on Wednesdays at prayer. Lynn introduced Randy Travis' song, "Keep Your Lure in the Water" which was a constant reminder of relying on Jesus.

In October 2006 after Patty was placed on Hospice, K.C .was reviewing her laptop files and found the following email from Patty that had been written while K.C. was in Florida that previous February.

"Okay I got the message loud and clear! But let me try to explain what I sometimes feel. I am so overwhelmed with despair that I do feel Jesus is asleep in my boat; I know deep down in the depths of my soul that he is with me, but at the same time the feeling of extreme aloneness envelopes me. It is so very hard to explain what I am feeling; my faith is there but my heart is broken. Sometimes I am also overwhelmed with the grief of realizing where I am, where I am headed, and most of all the memories of what my life used to be. And I guess I am sometimes numb. Somehow, though, God always finds a way to help me feel and accept the changes happening to me. I know for sure that not only is he beside me, he also gives me the miracle of friendship. Without that miracle every single day and all of the joys, rays of hope and sometimes sadness that comes with it, he finds a way through all of you to shine the light of hope upon me.

So what I'm saying is that sometimes in the darkness I know he is there but I forget to wake him up. But he sure has a way of reminding me that I don't have very far to reach if I just open my eyes and look to him. As the reflection in the previous e-mail said, "he may or may not calm the storms, but he will always speak peace to our hearts." In the things that you do every day, whether it be to remind me of who is awake in my boat or to open my eyes to see who is sitting next to me, your kindness and compassion helps me to face and rise above the trials that are so hard. For that there are no words to describe how truly grateful I am to have all of you in my boat!!! I love you all and I really believe that without you helping me to steer my boat, I would not be here today

Love and blessings to all of you, Patty"

The story continues. After forwarding the above email that October day, K.C. made another discovery. She said "I know you are all going to think I am really crazy. This morning when I was cleaning out the car (after I sent the first email today) I found a folded up church bulletin. I am always picking up meditations wherever I travel. When I read the front cover, I couldn't believe the subject of this meditation. 'We're in the midst of the sea, in a boat that seems fragile, and there are howling winds and enormous waves that threaten to capsize us.' But there is more. I then opened the page and it was from Holy Family Catholic Church in Booneville! The date is August 7, 2005 which was the weekend Bill and I were in Cincinnati for that wedding and we drove to Booneville on Saturday. Now how is that for Divine Intervention? Here is the full text:

> We're in the midst of the sea, in a boat that seems fragile, and there are howling winds and enormous waves that threaten to capsize us.

This is the life of every person at some point. Jesus is there to help us negotiate the trials and as long as we keep our eyes on him, we can walk on water; that is, we can do the impossible. When we focus on the strength of the winds and the depth of the waves and how wet and cold we are, then we panic and grasp and clutch and – sink. When we give up our life to the care of Jesus, we save our life. When we grasp and clutch, we lose it. This is the truth Jesus taught us over and over again."

*[Printed with permission by Paige Byrne Shortal
with Liguori Publications, Inc.]*

More recently, K.C. shared her insight, "What a gift for me to find or rediscover this email transaction when she was placed on hospice care! It truly was Patty's way of talking to us maybe one last time after all. And one more amazing thing, the day that Patty was buried was January 28th which was the same day of this original reading."

I don't believe in happenstance. Through faith I believe that God has a hand in all things.

Chapter 13

*Now faith is being sure of what we hope for
and certain of what we do not see.*

HEBREWS 11:1

D id you know that the word faith is mentioned twenty
eight times in Hebrews Chapter 11? That is a fact that
my Bible-reading mother left in her journal to me. To be
sure of the accuracy, she also underlined the words in her
Bible in order to count them. This made it quite clear to her
that having faith must be an extremely important aspect of
life. I believe that is also why she felt a closeness to Patty,
since Mother saw the difficulty of her trying to live her faith
while dealing with a deadly and debilitating disease.

Two definitions of faith per The Merriam Webster
Collegiate Dictionary are: ". . . a firm belief in something for
which there is no proof and complete trust. . . ."[14] It sounds
similar to the description given by the author of the book
of Hebrews. St. Augustine described it as "Faith is to believe
what we do not see; and the reward of this faith is to see what
we believe."[15] However, many questions can be asked about

faith. If you are a faith-filled person, is there room for any doubts? Does faith mean you are always on the right path with no turns in the road? If we believe through our faith that God will answer our prayers, why do we not always see those answers? Are there different degrees of faith? If we are true believers in God, does that mean we should never be angry with Him or our circumstances?

I am not a theologian and am unable to answer these questions. I can only speak from experience. Patty believed that I was such a faith filled person. She based that belief on the fact that I could pray fairly fluently aloud. I laughed at her and told her that as a young Protestant, unlike Catholics, I was taught and expected to pray aloud and therefore that is why it came easily for me. I then shared with her some challenging times in my life when I had been unable to pray due to anger and remorse; but in Romans 8:26, we are told, "the Spirit helps us in our weakness. We do not know what we ought to pray for, but the Spirit himself intercedes for us with groans that words cannot express."

I have never doubted the existence of God or his son Jesus our Savior. But there have been times when I have been unsure of the direction He was leading. I think Patty was also searching for an answer as to why she had been afflicted with this disease. What meaning was this journey supposed to have? She had prayed for healing, but that did not seem to be God's answer. Just as Thomas needed affirmation when he saw the risen Lord, she wanted affirmation that there was a reason she was going through this trial. It was not Patty's nature to blindly accept it. Paul Tounier has been quoted as saying, "He who has never doubted has never found true faith either," which seems to echo Patty's reflections.

Sharon Salzberg, one of America's leading spiritual teachers and authors, believes that "Faith doesn't mean the absence of fear. It means having the energy to go ahead, right alongside the fear." [16] Faith is not just a belief, it is an action. But it also doesn't come as one big whoosh! Faith occurs through small steps as we gain a more mature understanding of God. If we look at individuals in the Old Testament, we find that their faith matured over many years. It took Moses forty years to get to the Promised Land. Sarah was ninety when she had the child God had promised her, it was unwavering faith that made Abraham take Isaac to be sacrificed when tested by the Lord, and Noah had to trust God's word that it would only be 40 days of floating around in the ark! One of the greatest leaps of faith occurred when Mary, a young teenage virgin, told the angel Gabriel, "I am the Lord's servant. May it be to me as you have said . . . ." (Luke 1:38) when told that she would give birth to the Son of God. At that point she surrendered her life to God's purpose. Similarly, Joseph followed the angel's directions and took Mary as his wife knowing that she was pregnant. They all took that step because they had a relationship with God that grew just the way ours can. After finding Patty's email about Jesus in the boat, K.C. shared: "It made me happy that she didn't really feel so alone on this journey and that her faith was really stronger than I could see from the outside looking in. But then, how does any one of us really know how strong someone else's faith is?"

My Mother's insightful journal has held many treasures that have helped me to reflect on the concept of faith and trust in regards to Patty. Her journal includes several teachings of the well known Baptist minister, Charles Stanley. A pertinent point that she wrote about instructs us to "weigh your faith on the scales of adversity." She continued by giving Rev. Stanley's clarification of the meaning of adversity, "Adversities are the difficulties we go through. Sometimes we can't understand why God puts us through them; and we may never know until we get to the other side." She also noted that "God knows how much we can endure. We may think we know; but He does know. We must remain faithful, even though we do not understand it." June Scobee Rogers, the widow of astronaut Dick Scobee who was killed on the space shuttle Challenger, gives this insight on faith, "When there are no answers, there is God".[17]

I shared my favorite Bible verse with Patty, "For I know the plans I have for you," declares the Lord, "plans to prosper you and not to harm you, plans to give you hope and a future" (Jeremiah 29:11). One might think that this certainly did not apply to her situation! But the whole concept of God's love falls in the first half of the verse; He has plans for us. We only see the snapshot; God sees the big picture and that is where faith comes into play. As Patty's journey progressed, I think we saw glimpses of that big picture being drawn. The second half of the verse has to do with faith. Patty did have a future; it would be with God. Barb Swiecki had multiple discussions about faith with Patty and shares these:

> "I remember her talking about faith in relation to her mother's death and the yellow butterflies; how upset she was at the hospital after her mother died and while she and her dad were going home. There was a little yellow butterfly that kept flying around her, almost bugging her. Somehow she eventually came to realize that butterfly was her mom's way

of telling her that she was OK, that she was free now and with the Lord. Patty talked about that in Kentucky when Louise made us the crocheted butterflies and Patty ended up with a yellow one. There are no coincidences in life!!!! Her sharing her faith with all of us strengthened my faith.

She had wonderful faith in God at the end, I think. I talked and she nodded when we talked about going to see the Lord. I gave her several questions to ask and to work out a few things with God. She assured me (again with the nod) that she would take care of it."

Another email that K.C. discovered in her laptop files was the following story about "Two Horses" which she had sent to Patty, Allyson and I while in Florida that winter. It is written on a multitude of websites and I have tried to find its author to no avail. It is a touching story about faith, trust, and friendship:

"Just up the road from my home is a field, with two horses in it. From a distance, each horse looks like any other horse. But if you stop your car, or are walking by, you will notice something quite amazing. Looking into the eyes of one horse will disclose that he is blind. His owner has chosen not to have him put down, but has made a good home for him. This alone is amazing. If you stand nearby and listen, you will hear the sound of a bell. Looking around for the source of the sound, you will see that it comes from the smaller horse in the field. Attached to the horse's halter is a small bell. It lets the blind friend know where the other horse is, so he can follow. As you stand and watch these two friends, you'll see that the horse with the bell is always checking on the blind horse, and that the blind horse will listen for the bell and then slowly walk to where the other horse is, trusting that he will not be led astray.

When the horse with the bell returns to the shelter of the barn each evening, it stops occasionally and looks back, making sure that the blind friend isn't too far behind to hear the bell. Like the owners of these two horses, God does not throw us away just because we are not perfect or because we have problems or challenges. He watches over us and even brings others into our lives to help us when we are in need.

Sometimes we are the blind horse being guided by the little ringing bell of those who God places in our lives. Other times we are the guide horse, helping others to find their way. Good friends are like that… you may not always see them, but you know they are always there. Please listen for my bell and I'll listen for yours. And remember…be kinder than necessary, everyone you meet is fighting some kind of battle. Live simply. Love generously. Care deeply. Speak kindly…..

> Leave the rest to God."
> Author Unknown

In conclusion, I believe that our faith is a continuous pathway with obstacles in the road, curves that throw us into the ditch, and deep ruts that we get stuck in for awhile. It is from this hardship that our faith deepens, because it makes us more reliant on God. "Therefore, since Christ suffered in his body, arm yourselves also with the same attitude, because he who has suffered in his body is done with sin. As a result, he does not live the rest of his earthly life for evil human desires, but rather for the will of God" (I Peter 4:1-2). A wise person once said, "When there is nothing left but God that is when you find out that God is all you need." Patty's focus did change after her diagnosis. Her faith grew and became more real to her. During this process, we FLOPS also found that our own faith was solidifying and that our commitment to each other was increasing.

Chapter 14

I waited patiently for the Lord;
he turned to me and heard my cry.

PSALM 40:1

Then I said, "Here I am, I have come—it is written about
me in the scroll. I desire to do your will, O my God; your
law is within my heart. I proclaim righteousness in the great
assembly; I do not seal my lips, as you know, O Lord. I do
not hide your righteousness in my heart; I speak of your
faithfulness and salvation . . . ."

PSALM 40: 7-10

So with Aide #2 gone, the search was on for a replacement. Patty felt that it would be better for her to have a team of two-three aides to help rather than relying on (and getting attached to) just one. Mike and Patty made contact with Paulette, a resource person they became acquainted with through an aide Mike had hired when he had to be out of town overnight. Patty asked me to be a part of the interviewing process when Paulette brought four or five aides to the house to meet with them. The morning went well and we were not hesitant to ask specific questions regarding their experience with the special needs that Patty had; they probably thought they were being grilled! Within a few days decisions had been made. Some of the aides did not feel they were capable of doing the tasks required. After eliminating those, three were chosen. Patty thought that this would work well but there were definite issues. It was difficult to get a group "up to speed", so to speak, on Patty's routines, equipment and how she liked things to be done when they were not with her every day. Patty's speech was also beginning to be more slurred and she would have to repeat herself multiple times for them to understand what she was saying. This became frustrating to her since it occurred each time a different aide came. Even though this was her wish, it was not going as she would have liked, plus it seemed almost too impersonal. Carol Finucane joined the FLOPS around this period of time and recalls, "Patty had just lost her primary caregiver. There was a lot of tension, stories unknown to me, stress and anxiety. That was just before God sent Denise to be with Patty. In the meantime, it was a hodgepodge schedule of people spending time so Patty wouldn't be alone while Mike went to work."

About this time another aide approached Paulette and asked if she had any work for her to do since her last patient had just passed away. Denise had not met Patty with the previous group as she had a health problem that day. Paulette told her about Patty's situation and asked her to meet her and spend a few days to see how things worked. Patty knew immediately that Denise's skill level and demeanor were a good fit and so the idea of a team soon was defunct. She openly shared her experiences with the two previous health aides and both her physical and spiritual concerns for the last link of this journey. Denise understood; she "got it" because she too had a very strong Christian faith which she easily shared with others. Greg reminisces, "Luckily, in the end Denise was there. She was such an incredible person with her upbeat attitude and faith in God. At least in my eyes, it was a true blessing that she came to us when she did."

I talked to Denise while preparing to write this book. She told me that she felt God had placed her there with Patty and that she knew this from the beginning. With the experiences she has had with other patients, Denise believes "God uses me as a crossover and He allowed me to see Him through Patty." She had told Patty that she could say anything to her, and one day Patty actually was argumentative with her. During Patty's nap, Denise prayed about it and when Patty awoke she apologized to her. Denise told her it was all right because she was "commissioned to be there."

During this changeover, K.C. was in Florida (still emailing about Jesus in the Boat!) and so had not met Denise. Patty sent her the following email dated 3/3/06:

"All I have to say is this has been an incredible two weeks. I have trouble putting into words what has happened here since Denise has come into our life. It is a feeling I can't put my finger on. It feels very different than when (#1) or (#2) started here. There is a consistency and a familiarity like she knew me before she arrived. I don't even feel like she is new. What you see is what you get every day, no hidden agendas just plain truth and compassion and spirituality beyond all understanding. I can't wait for you to meet her. We have had wonderful conversations about our faith and trust and how you turn everything over. You know how I always want to take my marbles and go home, so we talked about that one

day. Well here is the part where you would say 'I told you missy, Jesus isn't comatose in your boat,' and I will say you were right on that one. Maybe I should listen to my friends a little more often huh?!"

The great religious philosopher Martin Buber has written, "When two people relate to each other authentically and humanly, God is the electricity that surges between them."[18] And so a new day dawned and the FLOPS were united in their belief that God had answered another prayer—with Denise.

Patty had also come to some other major decisions, and signing her Five Wishes document was one of them. She had avoided doing this previously. Why did she feel now was the time? I am not sure. Perhaps she knew she was getting weaker. Perhaps it was because her voice was diminishing and she was now using a microphone. The voice activated computer program was no longer working since it could not decipher the words due to the deterioration of her speech. Patty's computer was so important for her to keep in touch with family and friends that this was a major disruption. Greg installed a new computer program where she used the mouse to click on a keyboard to spell out words. This was definitely slower but she was still able to use the computer. It was obvious that she had signed the Five Wishes form previously since now she could no longer write, but only had it completed and dated at this time. Two of the FLOPS, Allyson and Peggy, witnessed it. It was a relief that this legal matter was completed and yet we were sad too.

- <u>Wish One</u> chose who her health care agent would be, Mike, and listed choices she wanted him to be aware of (quote):

1. *I do not want to be in a nursing home.*
2. *I would prefer to die in a hospice environment. But if it is okay with my children I would like to be at home.*
3. *If I have a medical emergency, I would like my doctors to keep me comfortable until my husband and three children can be with me.*

- <u>Wish 2</u> shared her wish for the kind of medical treatment she did or did not want:

  "I do not want CPR, major surgery, blood transfusions, dialysis, antibiotics or anything else meant to keep me alive. I do not want medical devices put in me to help me breathe or tube feedings meant to keep me alive for (an) extended period of time." She also chose not to have life-support treatment.

- <u>Wish 3</u> related to prewritten choices of how comfortable she wanted to be and things that could be done.

- <u>Wish 4</u> was a prewritten list of how she wanted people to treat her, and the final

- <u>Wish 5</u>, was a prewritten list of things she wanted her loved ones to know and specific funeral arrangements, such as the songs to be played.

Patty didn't avoid the subject of death. She was quite open in speaking about it. It had taken her two years to know in her heart that she did not want a respirator and tube feedings. I recall her saying something like, *"If I can't talk, can't interact, can't eat, and can't move, then why be alive."* At times she even found some humor, as this email to K.C. relays.

"I have this funny story to tell you. Lynn and I went

card shopping for the kids. You remember I asked her to help me pick out gifts and cards for each of the kids weddings and babies in case I am not here. We were looking at the wedding cards and we looked at one rack that I think were those Helen Steiner Rice cards. There was one that said 'my son' on it and we started to read it and both started to cry; as we looked away to wipe our tears the music in the store started playing 'On Eagles' Wings.' Lynn says 'oh my God' and we really started blubbering. We continued reading and the music went into the theme from 'Beaches,' so then we started to laugh. We picked up another card and the song went back to 'On Eagles Wings.' so Lynn looks up and says 'alright, alright we will buy the card. We don't need to be hit over the head; we are listening, we are listening!' Between the tears and the laughter I think they thought we were psycho! We both said we can't wait for K.C. to hear this one as she will never believe it."

As the spring of 2006 emerged in Pittsford, we saw changes in Patty's physical condition that left us wondering what was coming.

Chapter 15

Therefore, if anyone is in Christ, he is a new creation;
the old has gone, the new has come!

2 CORINTHIANS 5:17

Therefore we do not lose heart. Though outwardly we are
wasting away, yet inwardly we are being renewed day by day.

2 CORINTHIANS 4:16

Allyson decided that Patty needed something to occupy her time while at home; so she brought two Monarch caterpillars in a jar to the Stachura home, replete with milkweed leaves to feed them. Many of us had never seen this transformation into a butterfly and so it was the topic of discussion every day when a new FLOP appeared on the scene. One day when K.C. and Patty were out in the van, Patty wanted her to stop and get some more milkweed leaves for the caterpillars. As she wandered into a field of weeds, Patty, ever in charge, called out from the window *"Do you even know what milkweed looks like?"* Needless to say these were not endearing words to K.C. who retorted, "Of course I do!" We found it fascinating to watch the chrysalises being formed; all except Denise. She was not keen on having "creatures" in the house. The day that the butterfly emerged was memorable. Denise remembers that as the butterfly climbed to the top of the jar, Patty put her hand with the brace on it, up to the edge and the butterfly climbed onto her brace. She moved her hand and it just sat there for a long time.

One might surmise that there could be similarities between humans and butterflies. Within the chrysalis a transformation occurs to the caterpillar as it slowly matures into a butterfly. Throughout our lives, all of us wait for changes to occur, sometimes patiently and sometimes resignedly much like the caterpillar. Often these intervals bring us more in tune to the world around us. Mike wrote: "Patty's butterfly story was a gift from Allyson...the girls understood where Patty (or perhaps both of them) was in her spiritual transformative journey." Becky recalls "I remember the day a few of us sat around her kitchen table and quietly watched the butterfly emerge from its chrysalis. How slowly this process took place. Patty sat in silence and watched this small miracle happen. In hindsight I see it as the slow process Patty went through to escape the confinement of her illness and be freed to fly into God's loving hands."

This phase for Patty was marked by times of laughter and times of tears. She had gradually gotten to the point where she couldn't use the adaptive silverware and we had to feed her. Sounds like an easy thing to do....most of us have fed our children when small. However, timing the next bite, cutting things the correct size, putting the right amount into her mouth seemed like a slow motion movie with her directing and the FLOPS trying their best. We had to make sure we spread the jelly to the very edge of her toast; it was all about Patty being in charge! None of this stopped us from going out to eat. I often told her jokingly, that there was going to come a day when she couldn't yell at me anymore! In retrospect that likely sounds cruel, but she just rolled her eyes and laughed at me.

One evening when I was visiting, she told me she had had a particularly depressing and frustrating day. She was crying and rolled her wheelchair into the living room in front of the picture window. I felt so bad; all I wanted to do was give her a hug like I would do with any of my friends. Just imagine what it would be like if someone couldn't physically hug you. So I decided to do just that; I straddled the front of her wheelchair, leaned over and put my arms around her. As I stood there for a few minutes, she finally said she could just imagine what it would look like if a neighbor walked down the street and looked in. There I was with my butt sticking out as I straddled her! We burst out laughing and couldn't stop.

In May some of the FLOPS, including myself, headed off to Booneville on the annual women's retreat. While we were away, Allyson and Lynn took Patty to Highland Park where Rochester's annual Lilac Festival is held. Allyson recalls, "She insisted on having her arms and legs uncovered to get all the sun she could. It was quite warm and sunny, everything in bloom, bright with color. I remember we were worried about her getting sunburned, but she would hear nothing of it. She just forged ahead in her chair at full speed. It was a trick keeping up and she enjoyed every minute of that. We sat by the tulip bed near Highland Drive and had a breakfast of pastries, O.J. and coffee. It was simple and full, a perfect spring morning shared among friends."

Back: Connie, Cindi, Becky, Cindy, KC, Jennifer
Front: Karen, Sr. Marge, Barb

Back Left: Connie, Cindy. Center: KC, Karen, Bev, Allyson,
Cindi, Jennifer. Front: Barb, Patty, Becky

Patty so enjoyed being outside amidst the fragrant lilacs. K.C. had also planned a surprise for Patty while we were in Kentucky. She and a friend had worked out a webcast so that Patty would be able to see us live while we had our evening prayer service. We invited Millard and Louise who brought her guitar and sang for Patty. Sr. Marge had never met Patty and so she was able to do so. It was a very special emotional time for Patty to be able to share in the experience without actually being there.

As Patty's speech deteriorated there were questions of safety. This email was sent by me on May 19 to the FLOPS:

"Some of the FLOPS have concerns about caring for Patty alone at this point, since it is sometimes difficult to understand her and also difficult to know when she is short of breath on the lift. Obviously this is more noticeable when she is fatigued as well. There is concern about not knowing what to do if alone. We all know how frustrating it is for Patty as well. I am glad that this concern was voiced, as I am sure some of you have felt this way as well but have not mentioned it to me. Even she and I had some of those same issues on Monday when I was there. I want you to always feel comfortable in discussing concerns with me and if I can't help we certainly will work together with Patty and Mike.

I would like to try and schedule two people together if at all possible. Yes, that may mean an every week rotation rather than every other week for some people. Please let me know your thoughts and if you want to be doubled with someone. I will do the best that I can with the existing schedule. Again if there are certain dates at this point when you aren't available please let me know now. I have copied Mike into this note so he is aware of what is going on. I have not included Patty but obviously will be discussing it with her. Frankly, I believe she will feel more comfortable with two people as well.

Thanks for your love and concern. Major FLOP"

Denise continued to pray with Patty and to read scripture to her. Patty was so at ease and comfortable with Denise who truly was an expert at meeting her needs. Despite the differences in their religious upbringing, Patty was Catholic and Denise Baptist; they shared the common denominator of loving the Lord. Nevertheless, one day an event occurred that left both of them mystified; an event that rivaled "Jesus in the Boat" when it came to being discussed over and over.

It was an ordinary afternoon with Patty sitting in her usual spot at the kitchen table and Denise in the kitchen working at the stove or sink. Denise looked over at Patty and could tell that something was going on by the astonished look on her face. Patty sat there staring at a blue floral tissue box that usually was on the table for impromptu crying episodes. When Denise checked to see what was going on, Patty asked her if she could see the image of the Virgin Mary on the tissue box. I distinctly recall Patty telling me that Denise was a little "freaked out" because she did not see anything and couldn't quite comprehend what Patty was describing since she had no experience with Marian sightings! I also remember that both Patty and Denise said there was a certain peace that seemed to come over her. Patty did not hesitate to tell everyone about her visit. K.C. admits to being "a little doubtful but she really was adamant about it. And she was pleased to have had such a visit." The FLOPS analyzed that tissue box repeatedly but none of us saw the image. Needless to say, no one was about to throw the box away when it was empty either!

Patty was keen on listening to Christian music. The Wednesday prayer group became a threshold for multiple Christian groups to move our hearts; many filled us with inspiration and many made at least someone cry. Randy Travis was a favorite and the first time "When Mama Prayed" was played, I burst into tears. Of course I then had to explain how it seemed to mimic the family that I grew up in. It was easy to share confidences with these women who had become like sisters. Lynn described us, "We (The FLOPS) believe in the value of sisterhood, the strength and responsibility of being a woman, and the guidance of the Blessed Mother." Other favorite songs were about friendship — "Circle of Friends", faith — "Jesus Will Still Be There", "In the Calm", and "You are My All and All". I still listen to these songs whenever I need to be lifted up and whenever I need inspiration to keep writing Patty's story.

Patty began feeling very weak in July and she did not look well. Everything became an extreme effort for her. She went to see her medical doctor who found that she had a quite low potassium level and he put her on potassium supplements. For those who do not know, potassium is a very foul tasting medication and comes in either a very large pill or liquid form. She chose the pill; however, she was concerned about taking it for fear of choking. I was always anxious when she was taking her medications; she would put the pill in her mouth, take a large sip of water and throw her head back while swallowing it. It would also sometimes make her nauseated which was risky as well.

Having worked in Home Health Care, I suggested she ask for a referral for IV potassium as I knew that could be done and she certainly seemed like a prime candidate. For some unknown reason she deferred asking about this. She had lab work done weekly, I believe, but the supplements did not seem to be making any difference. We stopped going out for breakfast as she was just too tired. Given the importance of this ritual to Patty, it was obvious that she was starting a downhill slide.

Her father, who lived an hour away in Buffalo in a nursing home, was doing poorly. Patty had been unable to visit in several months as she was fearful of picking up a respiratory infection that could be fatal for her, so she talked to him on the phone as best she could. Daniel Beiter died on July 24, 2006 and Patty was heartbroken. She traveled to the wake in Buffalo for just a brief time, but didn't stay long since she wanted to conserve her strength for the funeral the next day. As several of the FLOPS sat in the church for the funeral, we wondered where she and Mike were. They arrived late, and we were to learn that they had to stop in order for Patty to use the NIV machine; the first time she ever used it outside of her bedroom. Patty was weakening and she knew it as she wrote the following letter to Dr Thornton:

"I am a train wreck (haha) everything seemed to go downhill about four weeks ago. The trajectory took a major nosedive. I started with the same symptoms that put me in the hospital last year. Then my father got sick with congestive heart failure and pneumonia so I could not go to see him. After a week he passed away July 24th. Then the wake and funeral in Buffalo and I became sicker. I saw my medical doctor, was put on potassium for a low level. He also found

a urinary tract infection, klebsiella pneumonae, was put on cipro twice a day but I only took it five days as it was awful.

My breathing sucks, when I was sick I used the NIV machine more. Now I use it 11 hours at night and about 2 hours for a nap. I use it to get on and off the toilet which Kim told me to do months ago.... but I'm just doing it now (haha). You know me.

Swallowing is a little more difficult. Taking some of my pills with applesauce and swallowing the rest for right now. I am pretty impressed with myself that I can swallow the potassium capsule, it's huge!

I am weaker in my shoulders, arms and neck. I am finding it hard at the end of the day to suck on a straw, and my head is heavy. I did not take my pills for two weeks because the potassium and Cipro added to my nausea and dry heaves. They also gave me Prilosec to help my stomach.

Feeling better on potassium 10meq/day. I see my doctor on Friday. I am back on most of my meds working my way up to 1200 mg CoQ10. I am not yet taking vitamin E, selenium, vitamin B12. I am feeling stronger this week but my stomach is still upset after taking the potassium.

My wishes have not changed, so any words of wisdom? Come on. I am counting on you to say something profound. So don't disappoint me.

On a lighter note, our son Dave is going to propose to his girlfriend on Friday and our daughter Alyson's boyfriend is also shopping for a ring.

I need help with the frustration of no one understanding me; ideas for an alphabet board or something. I've been trying to work with the (speech device) but you know what a bull head I am. (haha)"

Low potassium levels cause weakness and this was so

evident with Patty. One Saturday Aly called me from her mother's. She was alone and had tried two times unsuccessfully to get her mom in the lift to go to the bathroom. Patty suggested she call me and fortunately I was available. After the two of us were triumphant and got Patty settled for her nap, we walked into the hallway outside of her bedroom and Aly broke into tears. I just put my arms around her and hugged her. The kids were always so upbeat when they were with her, I think the realization of her current status was hitting home. I told Mike that night that Aly shouldn't stay alone with her anymore. Not surprisingly, many of the FLOPS had the same concern for themselves.

Chapter 16

Come to me, all you who are weary and burdened,
and I will give you rest.

MATTHEW 11:28

Patty's speech was very difficult to understand, she was very weak, and the FLOPS were concerned about her choking, as she did have some occasional difficulty with swallowing. In June, the speech therapist had set up an adaptive communication device which Mike described as "a small computer with multiple pull down menus that allows Patty to select and/or speak phrases or words. This tool can store several hundred phrases. We have not worked out all the details, but in all likelihood it will be mounted to the wheelchair and she will access it with the joystick for the chair (or some other control device). It is intended to make it easier for Patty to communicate with us as she always has." The concept was great; but Patty found it very slow and frustrating and it was never fitted to the wheelchair. Although she had had the device for months, she had not wanted to take the time to set it up and learn how to use it.

Now she became exhausted easily. Carol elaborates on how Patty was truly affected by the progression of her illness.

"Joining the FLOPS well into their journey with Patty often made me feel a bit disconnected, mostly because their journeys began so much earlier than mine and the gaps in understanding were large. Patty closed those gaps. She loved to laugh, to spend time at the kitchen table, to share her thoughts.

As time passed, sharing those thoughts became so much more difficult for her. Slowly, she lost her ability to communicate clearly with words. To the very last, she never lost the ability to communicate – very clearly – with her beautiful eyes. Patty had finally acquiesced to using the dreaded speech board. Her ability to communicate had been reduced to painfully and slowly formed words, laboriously tapping out letters and pre-selected words to share her deepest thoughts and most basic needs. Over the course of one long morning, Patty shared an enormous gift with me, and I hope I shared one with her. She told me how she felt that she was becoming lost in ALS. That people were seeing her and responding to her more as an object than a person, that they couldn't see her any longer. Sentences were finished for her – even when the idea she had been trying to express was incorrect. The mechanics of caring for her, getting the pills down, feeding, clothing, bathing left her on the outside. She struggled to communicate these thoughts and more.

Patty thanked me for listening, for being present and really trying to understand all of what she wanted to say. She thanked me for the gift of spending time to really hear what she had to say. All I had to do was be truly present and unconcerned about time passing. It is a gift Patty gave to me."

Since none of us were there on a daily basis, using the Stella lift did not come automatically for us. Frequently Patty would have to direct us and now she really couldn't. She occasionally became short of breath, and some questioned whether we were equipped to care for her safely anymore. The only good news at this point was the announced engagement of Dave and Ericka in August. Patty was absolutely thrilled and it seemed to give her a boost and stamina to push onward. As they began planning the wedding Dave recalls,

"Shortly after getting engaged Ericka and I started talking about locations and dates. We thought about a number of different options but eventually decided on Pittsford and getting married at Transfiguration with the reception nearby. We thought this would be the best option to make sure Mom could make it to the wedding and help her feel comfortable that she would be close to home rather than being at a hotel out of town. While doing some of the initial planning, I thought for sure that Mom would be healthy enough to be there. I knew that things were changing and figured the logistics of the day might be tough but I thought she would certainly be there. Then, Aly called me one day in Sept and told me that Mom had had a very difficult night. It seemed that in just a matter of a few days her condition was changing pretty significantly. That is when I first started thinking about the possibility of her not being at the wedding, which was a very difficult thought."

One evening I asked everyone to go to Patty's for Denise to review the Stella lift and to post directions on the bathroom wall. At this point it really did take two FLOPS to use the lift, one to operate it and one to help give her hips and buttocks firm support until her knees locked in place so that she could actually stand. After the demonstration the FLOPS met at my home for a meeting to review concerns. I asked Mike to come; I deliberately did not ask Patty to come as I knew that people would not be open and honest with her present. She was very upset with me as I knew she would be. She felt that we were talking about her behind her back and should have the courage to face her with our concerns. Instead of backing down, I told her that I would take exact notes and discuss everything with her that was said. I held to that promise.

Individuals were forthright in bringing concerns forward. The group discussed the risk of choking when she takes her medications, which was scary for Patty as well as for the FLOPS. Options presented included crushing the larger pills and putting the crushed pills in ice cream or sorbet. Mike instructed us on using the Cough Assist machine on exhale as an emergency measure. There is an Ambu bag in the van and a suction machine in the closet although it is mainly for superficial suctioning in the mouth, not throat.

Mike verified what should be done in an emergency in accordance with Patty's Five Wishes Document. Pittsford ambulance and Fire Department are aware of Patty's situation. We are to call 911, and then call Mike; Patty has said she wants short term support until the family is gathered and then they will take it from there according to her wishes.

It was suggested that perhaps we could have some outside help with meal preparation from neighbors and other church members who have asked to help in some capacity. I volunteered to ask Elaine Lotto, a neighbor, if she would help Lynn in coordinating meals. Patty later agreed that she would put together a list of food or menus that might work well for her and the family.

We wanted Patty and Denise to create a shopping list of things that we could pick up as needed to help take the load off daily shopping and evening trips for Mike. We also wanted to know how Patty would like us to spend our time with her: reading, going for walks, manicures/pedicures, foot rubs, watching a movie, listening to music, responding to email for her or whatever was personally important to her. We asked her to put a list together and the first thing she wanted to know was "Is anyone good at waxing (for her face)?"

We discussed how important it was to share information among ourselves such as not touching her back when she is standing or not leaning against the table, as her balance and equilibrium is very unstable. We all make mistakes during our time with her since we aren't professionals, but it was helpful to know some triggers.

One of the major topics was care giving and how comfortable Patty was with each of us caring for her and using equipment. We wondered if she would be more at ease with someone better skilled than ourselves and subsequently we would take a supportive role. Some of the FLOPS were more relaxed with care giving than others but Patty's opinion was what counted. This led to a discussion on how they would cope if we took less of a care giving role; either Denise would need to work more hours or they would have to hire another aide. Mike said this would be something that he, Patty and Denise would obviously need to talk about.

In conclusion, the group felt the following points were of utmost importance:

- We want to do what is safest, best, and wanted by Patty

- We need to evaluate our own personal level of comfort

- We encourage Patty to let us know her comfort level with each of us

- Asking Patty how she wants us to support her is vital (as an emotional/spiritual support, caregiver, or both)

- We will always be there for her, though perhaps in a different capacity

- All points raised by the group members are valid

After Mike left I told the FLOPS how truly important they had been to Patty and Mike, not just as a support system but financially as well. By Mike only needing to pay a nursing aide in the afternoons, the FLOPS had saved them at least $45,000 over these three years and had provided dinner every day for two of those years. This was a tremendous factor in the huge cost of ALS. I later calculated the total out of pocket cost for equipment/meds/and personal care through Mike's rough estimates, and it came to approximately $100,000+ not including the addition they put on their home. Truly the FLOPS were a gift to them in many ways.

The following day I discussed the meeting with Patty in detail; Allyson had taken notes and we went over each point and got her opinion. Mike responded with an email to me a few days later:

Dear Medical Director,

We have completed one of our homework assignments. Patty has agreed to the following schedule with Denise: Monday (because Cindy is available) and Wednesday (because it is prayer day): Denise 12:00 to 6:15 Tuesday, Thursday and Friday: Denise 8:00 to 6:15.

The FLOPS are still very much needed for fellowship and emotional support; if you want to schedule them that's great. If not, stopping in is great too. This schedule also provides the flexibility for them to visit in the afternoons. Patty is requesting a FLOPS team (2 FLOPS) for Monday and Wednesday (except somehow Cindy counts as a team).

Again thank you for all your support!!!!

We will now move on to assignment number 2. Mike

Although she certainly fussed and fumed for several days, Patty finally came to forgive me for holding the meeting without her. As a result of the meeting, it was evident that the role of the FLOPS would change.

Chapter 17

*As for you, go your way till the end. You will rest,
and then at the end of the days you will rise to receive your
allotted inheritance.*

DANIEL 12:13

Patty was losing weight; therefore a food and fluid diary was being kept. Since she was no longer feeling well enough to go out for breakfast, pancakes had given way to soft boiled eggs for the protein. No one could cook them correctly, although we all claimed to be the best until Patty told the next one that they just weren't quite perfect. She continued to amuse herself by playing us against each other.

As noted, I felt strongly that Patty and Mike should get rid of the dogs, Mulligan and Riley, when it was so easy for Patty to fall with a brush against her legs. During the journey I did change my opinion. Patty loved having the dogs as companions.....and the dogs loved having the FLOPS spoil them! Mulligan would go right into the bathroom and stay there with her, much to Denise's chagrin. They truly were a comfort to her.

Aly and Scott announced their engagement in September. Patty was excited to know that at least two of her children were finally getting married and there was also hope for Greg since he was dating Sara Beth! She joked with Barb that the only thing which really worried her was that very likely Aly would want to get married on a nude beach in the Bahamas and Mike would have to deal with that alone! Her sense of humor was unstoppable.

Finally in September Patty had a PIC (a special intravenous line inserted for long term access to give medications) line placed for intravenous potassium supplements since her level just could not be maintained on the pills. This required some special maneuvering and caution when lifting her with Stella so that it wasn't pulled out. She was also experiencing diarrhea which made quickness in our actions important as well. Thank God for Denise who had everything down to an incredible science! I sent the following email to the group a week after the PIC line was placed:

"Patty is looking and feeling better today, when I went up. She had been watching the Buffalo Bill's game and was sitting in bed watching the second half as we hooked her up. She even cracked a couple of jokes. Diarrhea is gone, still going very light on food today as a precaution but wanted to know what I was bringing for dinner tomorrow night and requested mashed potatoes. So you know she is feeling better. I think I am going up for a bit tonight so Mike can go out for coffee with Neil; which I think is a good idea, too. When I asked about it, Patty vehemently shook her head, yes, that he should go. Prayers are working, keep them going. Also I wanted to see what the interest from the FLOPS was for going to Geva to see 'Tuesdays with Morrie'. It says to bring your hankie but heck we are already living it. I just thought it might be good to share it. Barb, you asked about visitors, by all means, yes, she would love to see you I know. Cindy"

This rally was short lived. In early October, Patty went to the hospital and was diagnosed with pancreatitis. Hospitalization was an incredibly arduous experience for her as can be seen in Mike's email when she was released:

"Thank you to everyone for your prayers and concern. I think we passed through a low point yesterday and are now headed back in a good direction. Some day Patty can tell you about the hospital stay. It was an adventure. They are not equipped to handle ALS patients.

One sign that my Patty never really abandoned me through this adventure... on the way home from the hospital she was exhausted, on the NIV machine and generally almost in an unstable condition ... but she was strong enough to make a point as to the route she wanted to take home. No question she was piloting from the right chair as always!

Patty is on a clear liquid diet while her digestive system heals; okay I'm no doctor, that's the best I can do with details. She will likely be on IV's at home for a while as this is her main source of fluids. She is also experiencing some issues of shortness of breath; so she is using oxygen and trying some meds to help with these symptoms. Generally she is either on the NIV machine or oxygen, so don't be surprised to see the oxygen; I think it may now be a permanent part of our world. We will have daily visits from a nursing service for a while to take blood samples and monitor vitals to give the doctors an accurate view of her progress, so expect to see some unfamiliar faces here for a while. When she feels up to it she can tell you her nickname for the nurse.

Things were serious enough that Dr Thornton made a house call today. He was here for over an hour to check things out first hand. He provided several suggestions on next steps in treatment that were very useful.

Today Allyson and KC helped Denise get Patty back into her routine. It was a slow beginning but as always, when I got home from work I got back a Patty that was much better than the one I left in the morning..... Thanks Allyson and KC.

It's my recommendation that we hold off on a lot of visitors this week as its tough for Patty to communicate while using the NIV machine, and she now uses it a lot, and she is pretty pooped. She really loves to see you all but her batteries are kind of drained just now.

Thanks to all the FLOPs who participated in the shower for Denise on Wednesday. She was very touched. She is a very special person to our family and we appreciate how you guys treat her as part of the family. She was a huge help at the hospital on Friday.

Please know that your prayers are very special and certainly very effective. Your fellowship is so important to Patty that I truly think it is what has kept her from giving up on this difficult journey. Each new leg of this journey comes with an increase in challenges that we never know how we will meet... but you guys are a big reason we make it. I thank God every day for the blessing of bringing us the FLOPs. I know too many people on this journey alone and I do not know how they do it.

God bless you all.
Patty and Mike"

The hospital experience was horrific. The staff could not understand her when she explained what she needed. They had no concept of what WAS needed and they were so busy that they had no time to figure any of it out. Food and water were left on her tray in front of her but no one realized she needed to be fed. Her experience using a bedpan always led to a wet bed since she was dead weight when they tried to turn her. Worst of all, while giving her care some acted as though she had some mental incapacity, the one thing that made her the angriest! She was very frightened as well, knowing that her life was in their hands because she was so powerless. She was so glad to return home and vowed that she would not go back to the hospital again.

Despite the decline in her health, Patty still had her desire for control intact as well as her sense of humor. The nurse who came to the house to change the PIC line dressing became known as *"Floozy Mama"* because of the provocative way she dressed. Funny, I have no recollection of her real name. All of us who were nurses were taken aback but none more than Patty who definitely had an eye on her sterile technique!

K.C. journaled:

"I do remember being at the house when Dr. Thornton paid a house call to the Stachura home. It was shortly after her hospital stay and Patty was having some more breathing issues and the IV didn't seem to be increasing her potassium levels at all. I remember that before he came, some other nurse was supposed to come to evaluate her and Patty was worried about the nail polish on her toes! So she told Denise to tell me to take it off! I stood there using the nail polish remover and wondering why this was SO important that it had to be done right then! So at least her toe nails were clean when HE came to visit and it made her laugh when I reminded her about cleaning them earlier. (K.C. didn't know that they check the color of nail beds to evaluate oxygenation which is why Patty wanted the nail polish removed.) Anyway, I left the room while he visited with her....but then she asked for me to come back. They were talking about pain medication and she was adamant about no morphine. He did tell her that her breathing would be better but she said she wanted to be alert too. So they agreed on some other pain medication. She also told him in no uncertain terms that she would NOT go back into the hospital. It was much more comfortable at home and he agreed. So, as always, Patty was certainly in control."

Patty had fought receiving Enriched Care for quite some time, even though it is a program planned to be used early in a progressive or debilitating disease in order to provide services to help maintain quality of life. Lynn recalls, "Patty's final acceptance of Enriched Care was a HUGE step for her to make for so many reasons:

- She could baby-step her way to Hospice.

- She couldn't get a doctor to define how much time she had left; Enriched Care might change this.

- She understood that so many were worried about Mike (and the kids) and they might receive more support.

- Every turn with insurance was unpleasant and she had been fearful that they might face another bureaucratic battle by adding an additional service to her health care plan.

- It was difficult for her to meet and trust new caregivers."

I am not sure if she thought receiving this earlier would have shown she wasn't fighting hard enough or what the reason was. I do recall when she made the decision for no life support that she was fearful the kids would feel she had given up. K.C. shares, "I asked her one day if she was afraid of death or the actual act of dying. Her answer was '*No, I know there is a heaven.*' I pressed her and said (as only I can, I guess) but that's not what I asked. I know if I were walking in your shoes of course I would be afraid of the dying process. Her comment was basically final... Don't go there anymore...when she said: '*I am afraid to leave everyone here behind.*'" So given Patty's weakening condition, I felt that Enriched Care was just a short precursor to Hospice.

On October 19th a friend from out of state emailed me to ask how Patty was doing. My reply:

"She is doing very poorly; she is very weak today and was in bed most of the day. She has a urinary tract infection and has been nauseated and dizzy, maybe from the antibiotic. I just got back from helping her husband lift her onto the bedside toilet as she was too weak to be up in the lift long enough to take her into the bathroom. She also told us that she wants to die…. I am close to the point of changing my prayers after seeing her this way. Is that awful of me? Or just merciful? Cindy"

Patty chose hospice on October 21, 2006 with Mike, myself and Dr. Thornton's Nurse Practitioner, around her bedside. After the NP left, I held her hand and tearfully leaned close to her and told her I had a burning question I needed to ask, "Should I look for butterflies or cardinals to know that you are with me?" She clearly said *"Cardinals!"* Patty's one request….that she never be left alone.

Chapter 18

Do not let your hearts be troubled.
Trust in God, trust also in me. In my father's house are
many rooms; if it were not so, I would have told you.
I am going there to prepare a place for you. And if I go and
prepare a place for you, I will come back and take you to be
with me that you also may be where I am going.

JOHN 14:1-3

As Patty turned things over to God, so did the FLOPS. Our role had changed and now we were praying for peace in this final journey for our dear friend. I continuously sent out updates to the FLOPS. This one was written on October 25, 2006.

"Today was an emotional day; Mike said he thought Patty had a better day than Sunday. Dave made a day trip home from Boston for the afternoon to see her. She was up in the chair this morning and this afternoon for about 30 minutes I think each time. Taking a few sips of tea. Mike did not go in to work today since Dave was home; I do not know about tomorrow.

Mike did share with me that he wanted us to write down good memories with Patty and for us to share these with her (see you should have kept those memory books I gave you!). He thinks that will lift her spirits some rather than her lying there feeling depressed; we do get a laugh (or smile) out of her occasionally. He also said they might be used later (which I am assuming is the funeral service).

Mike also wants us to know that when he is not there, Denise is in charge and we are to follow her directions since she knows most of what Patty wants. Denise definitely needs help in getting Patty up with Stella, as someone needs to "spot" her in the front with her head and chest so that she doesn't lean too far forward when going up. Someone also needs to "spot "her from behind as she sits on the edge of the bed so that she doesn't fall backward....
Don't lean on or put your knee on the bed, however, as that throws her backwards, and she still doesn't like you to hold onto her unless needed. Please just follow her lead. Thanks for your continued prayers and support during this difficult time."

Dave reflected on what went through his heart and mind as he drove home from Boston to see his mother.

"It seemed so hard to believe that one week I was thinking about Mom being at our wedding ... to getting a call on a Saturday night (in September) from Aly and then my Dad saying that Mom had taken a major turn. Ericka's family was in town for the weekend to do some wedding dress shopping and hang out in Boston. I went from having a great weekend with them and celebrating a big win by the BC football team to crying uncontrollably. Dad told me that the doctors thought it could be anywhere from a few days to a few weeks. I was completely devastated and had no idea what to do; should I wait for the following weekend to go home or should I come in sooner than that. I wanted one last opportunity to see Mom and hopefully talk with her and I was afraid if I waited I might not get that chance. I could not imagine not getting that last opportunity, so after talking to my Dad on Sunday, I decided I would get up early Monday and come back for the day. As I drove back early that morning, a lot of things went through my head from how unfair this disease was … to all the great times we had together, just the two of us and as a family. It was probably the only time that I have taken that six-hour trip that I was not in a hurry to get there. I felt like the quicker I got there; the time she had left with us would disappear faster.

I spent two-three hours there with Mom, Dad, you, and Denise. Mom wanted to get out of bed and after a lot of effort she made it to the kitchen table. We tried to talk a little bit but it was very difficult because you could see how incredibly weak she was. It was hard to know what to say because there is nothing to prepare you for that day or the realization that this might be the last time you see and talk with your Mom. While she said very little I knew how happy she was to see me. I got to spend fifteen or twenty minutes with Mom, just the two of us after she went back to bed. I was able to tell her a lot of things and thank her for all that she did for me, Aly and Greg, how important she was to all of us, and most importantly how great of a Mom she had been; that she had taught us so much and had such a huge impact on who all of us are today.

The drive back that night was so difficult, knowing that could be the last time I would ever see and talk to her. It turned out that would not be the last time, as Ericka and I came back the following weekend. But I did not know that would be the case, at that moment. Those next six hours I again thought about all of the good times we had together and how unfair it was for her, for my Dad and the rest of us that she was being taken from us so soon."

K.C. updated the group on Friday October 27th:

"Ladies: I know all of you are looking for some news about Patty. I spent some time this morning with her before the kids arrived. She seemed peaceful and comfortable; opening her eyes to pay attention when Mike and I talked to her. I followed Mike's request and left when all of the kids got there. Peggy spent some time in the afternoon helping Patty's sisters clean the refrigerator and trying to keep the house 'peaceful and somewhat quiet.' Peggy added that I should 'just tell people that Patty is happy to have her children and family around her, that she is relatively comfortable, and that she is aware of what is going on around her.'

As we continue to pray for a peaceful transition

for Patty, one thought keeps coming to my mind: 'All in God's time'. Patty will know when to row that boat toward the light. She knows we love her by the way we were with her every day in her struggle. And I know she loves every one of us because we stuck by her side along the way."

That weekend proved to be a very special time for Patty to be with her family. She was still alert and with Mike's help she was able to tell them how much she loved them and all of her hopes and dreams for them. She also gave each of them a very special gift, a quilt that she had asked Kim Cawley, her respiratory therapist to make. The amazing part of each quilt is that in the center was the inscription, *Love you, Mom*, in Patty's own hand writing taken from a card she had sent Aly long before her diagnosis. Kim sent a letter to each of the kids telling the quilt story.

October, 2006

"Dear Aly, Greg and Dave,

By this time, I'm sure that you have received the quilts I made. I wanted to write down the story behind the quilts so you would understand how much of your mother is in each of them.

I was at the house this past April and we were talking about the three of you (as we often did). Your mom was grumbling about how none of you were engaged and how Aly and Dave had potential fiancées but no rings yet. We also talked about her mortality, and how she wanted to have things for the three of you that were from her personally. I offered to make quilts. I came over the next week with an assortment of patterns, and some pictures of quilts I had made in the past. Your mom picked out a quilt pattern that I had made for my children. We then made plans to go to the fabric store together. We met at the fabric store and it didn't start out as a good day for your mom. She had just received a voice amplifier to use and wasn't happy with another new piece of equipment. I think she was also tired from getting out of the house on what ended up being an overcast and rainy day.

I had your mother close her eyes and think of each of you individually and pick a color that reminded her of you and your personalities. We were in an aisle next to the greens and she picked out Dave's colors first. She then went on to pick every piece of fabric in each of the quilts. It was amazing but as

Patty and Kim Cawley

soon as she started picking out fabric, she brightened up and, I know, really enjoyed the active role she was taking in this project. I've been sewing for a long time and I don't think I would have picked any different colors than what she did that day.

Next were the pictures that I copied onto fabric for the quilt. I didn't think I was ever going to get all the pictures for each quilt. She'd send me one or two and then change her mind. I was amazed at the detail of the pictures she picked and how most of them picked up colors from the quilts! Greg's graduation gown is a perfect example of this.

The inscription in the center came from a card that Aly had in her room from a long time ago. Your mom's friend, Peggy helped a lot with that one. I guess the original was on some sort of printed background. So there was a lot of cleaning up she needed to do so that I could easily transfer the words to white fabric. Your mother even told me what color to print each inscription with!

I guess the most important thing for you to know about these quilts is that I only sewed them together. Your mother, inspired by her love for you created each of them personally.

God has blessed you and I know he will continue to do so.

With love, Kim Cawley"

The kids took turns spending the night in her room so she would not be alone and this also gave them important 1:1 time with her. On October 27th, after talking with the kids, Patty requested that IV fluid be discontinued and all hydration stopped. She would only continue to receive her pain medication. On October 30th, I sent the following email to the FLOPS.

"Patty seems very comfortable; she continues to get pain medication and anxiety medication at regular times. I guess this morning she had her eyes open for awhile but most times has them partially closed. She hears and is aware of what is going on. Mike said she definitely knew when her brother Danny and Chris were in the room to tell her they were going back to Florida today. Carol, the Hospice nurse continues to say the end will likely come soon but it also appears that Patty as always is remaining in control of her departure. It was undetermined if Dave and Ericka were going back to Boston tonight or staying... a very difficult decision. The kids seem at peace and have had much individual time with her over the weekend. Several other family members also came to town.

Mike shared that he has had several calls about visiting (not just from FLOPS) and at this time his wishes are not to stimulate Patty too much and so is limiting visitors. This even includes some of the family. He is not doing this because of not caring about our concerns but rather, he feels it is better for Patty as she makes her journey. Patty knows how much we love her and will miss her and just as we always have, we need to think of her needs rather than our own right now. We have spent three years with her; it is our time to respect those wishes.

Mike and I have discussed the possibility of me giving a short reflection from the FLOPS at the funeral. I feel honored to do this and would like some input from all of you that I will try to incorporate. I would like to reflect on how Patty has changed our lives in how we feel about the following areas: Family/Friendship, Laughter, Opportunity, Perseverance, and Spirituality, another acronym for FLOPS."

Carol Blank, the hospice nurse who came to the house, had cared for ALS patients in the past. She was very attentive to Patty and was amazed at the support system that she had in the FLOPS. She told everyone at her agency about the FLOPS and what we had been doing for Patty for three years. She could sense the camaraderie, the love, and the spirituality of the group and later became a part of the Wednesday Prayer group in order to have some of the peace that she saw in us.

Denise became even more important to Patty if that is possible. We had known from the moment Denise entered the Stachura household that she was indeed the right person to be there for the final part of the journey. We continued to see that affirmation in all that she did for her. Much of her time was now spent sitting with Patty and praying or reading the Bible to her. At this point it took two people to help with her personal care since she was bed bound; and I am sure much to her total disgust, the Depends were now in place. Turning her was painful and she often grimaced or let out a small moan. Hearing this brought Mulligan right to the side of the bed and literally Denise had to push him out of the room at times.

Mike and I would split some night shifts whenever I wasn't working. One night while Patty was still somewhat alert, I arrived at 11pm with my nurse's cap on. I told her that the head nurse was on duty, I had some knitting that I wanted to do and I wasn't going to take any crap from her. She just rolled her eyes like she always did. On November 1, the FLOPS received the following update.

"KC told you about Patty perking up for Denise; I actually thought she seemed a little more alert today as she moved her head, yes, when I asked if she wanted pain medicine. Mike mowed the yard which was probably good to get him out of the house. He also took a nap this afternoon while I was there for awhile. I stayed part of the night last night for Mike to sleep and played the CD that Lynn had made of many of the songs that we listen to. I even sang to her (probably much to her dismay I am sure). She was probably thinking, 'How am I supposed to rest peacefully with this character singing to me.' She knew it wasn't the angels for sure!

Denise and I cleaned her up a bit today but I still told her she looked awful and that she must just be waiting for those white angel wings to be ready; or better yet maybe they are going to be red like cardinal wings. I thought she smiled. I figure that I have razzed her during this whole journey so she wouldn't expect any less of me now.

I don't think she has had any urine output since last evening according to Mike. He said the Hospice nurse said she may not make any more. Greg, Aly and Sara Beth were looking through pictures tonight choosing some for the funeral service, I guess. I think the kids have moved to that accepting stage and we need to thank the Lord for that. I have received some beautiful notes/memories/thoughts/ incidents from several of you; please send me anything that has made you smile and touched your hearts. I probably won't incorporate the leopard panties, though.

I love each and every one of you. Please don't hesitate to call me to talk in the evenings. Cindy"

It was complicated telling the FLOPS that Mike only wanted a few people there. They had come so far with Patty to not take this final walk with her. Those who could not be with her sent emails, such as this one from Becky:

"Dear Patty,

I prayed for you today asking Jesus to hug you and comfort you. I told Him to keep his arm around your shoulders and gently lead you to His home where you can forever look down upon your loving family and your friends. We all love you and will continue to be your friends. Please continue to be our friend guiding us in our quest so we too can reach it as you are."

Sue especially had a difficult time accepting this as she felt strongly that she needed to say goodbye. She shared with me that she had never been close to someone who died before and it was really difficult. I told her she should call Mike and ask if she could visit, and of course he said she should. November 4th email:

"Sue, Mike said he thought Patty enjoyed your visit yesterday afternoon. I am glad that you could go and am sure that it gives you more peace. I was up late last evening with Neil, and other friends arrived about the same time (not planned) to pray the rosary, so that was very touching for all of us to sit in the room praying. Gee my second time in twenty-six years saying the rosary.....what that Patty can do for us. Love, Cindy"

Alone at night with her I could sing, cry, cry while singing and just tell her how much I was going to miss her. It was such a special time for me. I even read her the reflection that I wrote for the funeral mass. I wanted her to know just how much she was loved and how she had transformed our lives.

Mike was exhausted. Two-three hours of sleep at night, continuous people coming through the house, nonstop phone calls and updates, and a deep apprehension that Patty might be in pain. Each day he heard the same words, "It shouldn't be much longer" and each day brought more anxiety as to whether she was hurting. The journey had been grueling; now was the time that he only wanted a merciful departure for his beloved Patty.

On Monday, November 6, 2006, I jotted down the following note:

"Today while I was there Mike went for a run. I am trying to encourage him to take a nap. He wouldn't today, saying he was fine. Be aware that his fuse is a little short sometimes; he is so concerned that Patty is not comfortable.

Mike just called to update me: Dr. Thornton was supposed to come today but couldn't and plans to come tomorrow. Mike updated him and talked quite awhile on the phone with him. He was surprised that Patty is still responding to pain stimulus (which I can verify she is when I turned her today) and so they have doubled her doses which will obviously make her more sedated. Dr. T. also said it is unusual for patients to survive after fourteen days once hydration is stopped; that date is on Thursday. He thought we would see substantial changes over the next twenty-four hours and then more so over the following twenty-four hours. But that is all he could speculate on until he sees her.

Mike has also said that it is OK for our prayer group to come to the house on Wednesday and pray around her bedside (as long as we are not rambunctious). I just felt this need today to ask him about this and he felt Patty would want that."

On Wednesday, November 8, 2006, the prayer group gathered in Patty's bedroom, along with Mike, Barb, Denise, and Hutch, for our usual Wednesday prayers which had been disrupted for at least a month. For some it was a time to reflect and say goodbye once more, for others it was a time to ask for grace. That evening, with Mike and Aly in the room with her, Patty went to join the Lord. We once again prayed the rosary at her bedside as we had the previous evening.

Chapter 19

.....God is faithful, and he will not let you be tested beyond your strength, but with the testing he will also provide the way out so that you may be able to endure it.

I CORINTHIANS 10:13
(NEW REVISED STANDARD VERSION)

Patty had told Mike that she did not want any calling hours at the funeral home prior to the funeral mass. Instead she wanted people to come and fill the church! *"Bus them in if you have to!"* A Saturday funeral mass was perfect for having a crowd … and she did …. 600+ people.

The night before there was a small private wake for family, FLOPS, and a few close friends who mingled and talked. To close the evening, Mike asked Karen to lead the group in the rosary just as we had for several nights at Patty's bedside. Mike also told us that he wanted the FLOPS to take the van to the funeral and that we would be the first vehicle after the hearse in the funeral procession.

All of us piled into the van, meaning several of us sat on the floor. As we arrived at the Church of the Transfiguration, we unloaded using the ramp. We left the ramp open as well as the front passenger door where Patty's wheelchair was always buckled in. On the floor was a single red rose.

The entrance hymn was "Gather Us O God," the song the women always used when we gathered for evening prayers while on retreat in Booneville, Ky. The first reading was from Philippians 4:4-7, the Second reading was from I Corinthians 10:13, and the Gospel Reading was Luke 24:13-16, 28-35. Deacon Mike Piehler, a close friend of the family, delivered the following Homily:

Mass of the Resurrection for Patty Stachura November 11, 2006

"Good Morning. On behalf of Patty's family, thank you all so much for being here this morning. Leave it to Patty to get us all out of bed so early on a Saturday morning and make us come to Church! But this is just what Patty really wanted – to be surrounded by her family and her friends, all together here at the Table of the Lord.

Michael, to you – Patty's ever faithful husband for twenty nine years; to you, Dave, Aly and Greg—Patty's three beautiful children; to Patty's brothers and sisters and extended family—on behalf of myself, Fr. Mike Bausch our Pastor, Deacon Will Johnson, the entire Transfiguration staff and everyone in the Church this morning—please accept our most sincere and genuine sympathies on your loss. But please accept this, as well. Please accept from all of us our deep and abiding belief and unshakable conviction that one day YOU WILL SEE HER AGAIN!

As most of you know, in December of 2003, Patty was stricken with ALS—known by many as Lou Gehrig's disease. Having watched her suffer with this disease, as it gradually paralyzed her, I could not help but think that this disease, in many ways, is a modern day crucifixion as it slowly robbed her of her ability to move, to swallow, to speak and finally to breathe. In fact, during the last several months of Patty's life, as her ability to verbally communicate was gradually taken from her—I believe this was her greatest suffering.

And so, last night, while the Stachura family was at a private wake for Patty—my wife Kathi, and I sat at the Stachura family kitchen table. I sat at Patty's usual place at the table and prayed to her about what I might say to all of you this morning at her Mass of Resurrection. I believe this is what she would have me say.

First of all—Mike, since Patty is no longer here and cannot buy your clothes, I know she is concerned that you're going to let yourself get frumpy. Patty doesn't want you to embarrass the family name.

Michael, in all seriousness, Patty wants you to know that she is at peace and loves you more now than ever before if that is possible. I believe she chose today's first reading just for you Mike. Hold onto this reading from St. Paul as a spiritual love letter between you and Patty. In spite of all that the two of you have been through, Patty calls on you to do as this reading says, "Rejoice in the Lord always, I say it again, rejoice. Everyone should see how unselfish you are." Michael that is not a demand of you, it is Patty's description of you….UNSELFISH. For if you have been anything, you have been an unselfish spouse and Patty wants you to know how incredibly grateful she is for having you as her husband, as her lover, as her very best friend.

And to you Dave, Aly and Greg, I believe your Mom wants me to tell you how proud she is of each of you and how much you have grown these past three years as each of you has dealt with her suffering in your own way and in your time. Her message to you is clear—Do not be afraid because she will always be with you. Dave, Aly and Greg, may I suggest this to you –pray TO your Mom because today she is a member of the communion of saints. Her love for each of you will always be there to wrap around you just like those quilts she had made just for you.

And by the way, don't forget Dad—keep in touch with him and check out how he's dressed—keep an eye on him for her.

And finally to all of us here this morning, Patty would tell us how important it is for each and every one of us to "know what matters," to know what and who really counts. She would tell us that we don't have time to brood or have self pity—because love, you see, expects so much more from us and love is all there is—in the end, love is all we have. Patty understood that.

Patty would tell us that Faith, Family and true Friends are the real source of our courage. She would tell us there are angels among us as she herself experienced with the FLOPS, an extremely dedicated group of women who cared for Patty daily for years (FLOPS- Friends and Loved Ones of Patty Stachura).

Today's second reading from Corinthians is taped to the wall above the toilet paper holder in Patty's bathroom and perhaps best describes the FLOPS—"God will not let you be tested beyond your strength. Along with the tests, God will give you a way out of it, so that you may be able to endure it." So often, Patty's "way out of it" were those FLOPS and, I must add, her aide, Denise. Patty's message to us all is that in spite of what we are called to endure we will never be tested beyond our strength.

Allow me to share with you a little story about a place that was very special to Patty, it is Holy Family Parish in Booneville, Kentucky. It has become a Holy Place for so many members of our parish, both men and women, who travel there each year on a retreat to work with the poorest of the poor in Appalachia. According to her husband, Mike, Kentucky, its poor, and the Franciscan nuns who serve there played a major role in renewing Patty's faith.

After having gone on retreat to Kentucky four times, Patty was physically unable to make the trip this past spring. She was so sad and disappointed because she knew that she would never see Kentucky again. However, K.C. Legg and another friend of our parish surprised her by setting up a web-cam, a video conference, so that Patty could participate live in night prayers each evening with all the women in Kentucky. Louise, a Kentucky mountain woman who suffers from severe bouts of depression, became a soul friend with Patty over the years and came to Holy Family Church for the express purpose to play her guitar and sing Patty's favorite hymns over the web-cam. There are Angels among us, indeed.

My dear brothers and sisters, Patty Stachura was no pie in the sky believer. The integrity of her spirituality was clear to all who met her. She had her feet firmly planted on the ground and that is where she expected God to be—right here with each and every one of us through thick and thin. Patty was relentless in her pursuit of God's promise to be with us always. She would not let Him off the hook. Patty was a woman with a Faith so tenacious that she demanded to know "where in the hell God was in all of this suffering?"

Well, Patty found her answer in today's Gospel. Like the disciples on the road to Emmaus, Jesus is always with us, but we just don't see Him all the time. That is why we are called to the tables of our lives—the kitchen tables of our homes, the kitchen table of ministry of Kentucky and the Table of the Lord—to break bread together and come to see Him once again in our loved ones that surround us. That is where the Lord will be found, you see, in our love for each other. And it was into the arms of that love that Patty surrendered in her final days. She rested in the love of her husband, the love of her children, the love of her friends and caregivers. She rested in the love of the Blessed Mother with whom she had a special relationship, one Mom to another.

My dear brothers and sisters, during the past several weeks, this parish, for all practical purposes has held a vigil, awaiting Patty's death. Today that vigil ends. Today we no longer speak of wheelchairs, paralysis or suffering. The crucifixion is over and Patty lives.

Today we celebrate a woman of incredible courage. Today we celebrate a woman of tenacious faith. Today we celebrate a woman who believed deeply in the sacredness of family and the joy of true friends. Today we celebrate a woman who called forth from this parish, its gifts, its generosity, its Faith and above all, its Love.

Patty Stachura you have run the race, you have kept the Faith, and you have endured. Now the crown of victory is yours – well done, good and faithful servant, well done."

The Offertory Hymn was "We Remember" and the communion Hymn, "I Am the Bread of Life." Next Dave and Greg gave a reflection; Aly stood with them but knew she would not be able to speak.

Dave's opening

When we think of Mom we could recount lots and lots of stories:

- Her colorful language screaming at the TV during Bills games.
- Her helping with homework after we waited until the last minute… except for math. It was dangerous to ask Mom for help with math.
- The constant question about when Ericka and I and Alyson and Scott were going to get engaged.
- The smiles and tears she had when we both finally did.

There are many stories we could tell but there are three things that we will always remember most fondly about Mom:

- Her support
- Her teaching
- And the fact that she always wanted the best for her children.

Our Mom always wanted the best for each of us. No matter what it was, school, sports or just about life, Mom did everything she could to make sure the best thing happened for us.

Our Mom would give us just the right amount of rope. She would never let us go too far and get into serious trouble. Mom would allow us to make our mistakes because she knew that we would learn from them and she was right. Right up until her final days, Mom was still teaching us. She taught us all about what it was to really fight as she battled

ALS. Mom showed us that it was okay to depend on others for help. Mom taught us about the importance and strength of marriage and a deep belief and faith in God.

Let us share a few short stories about Mom

Greg
When her father moved into an assisted living facility sixty miles away she visited him often. Frequently, especially around the holidays she had Grandpa stay with us. During each visit there would come a time or two where Grandpa would become confused or have issues with personal hygiene that caused a bit of a mess. Mom knew he did not mean to cause a problem; she always protected his dignity and without fanfare or embarrassment to him she simply cleaned up.

Dave
Our Mom was a tireless supporter of all three of us. She was our number one fan for every sport. Whether it was high school crew, lacrosse, hockey, soccer (high school and college), golf, softball, or all of the various travel and club teams the three of us played, Mom was always there. You always knew she was there because you could hear her in the stands. During her college soccer career, Aly always knew Mom would be in the stands even if it required a four-hour drive to watch a two-hour soccer game. Mom thought her countless hours of watching us play certified her to be referee so she was always willing to help any ref with a call.

Greg
When she began to use the power wheelchair she sometimes ran over Fr. Mike's toes during communion. We are not

sure, but think this might have been a commentary on the homily of the day.

Dave

Mom was always buying cards and little gifts for friends and family to celebrate successes or just let them know she loved them. The cards had to communicate the perfect message and took awhile to select. Dad thought she secretly owned stock in a major card company. Very often the recipients would be so touched that they would end up in tears.

Greg

Boonville Kentucky was a special place for mom. She went to Kentucky with the women of Transfiguration four times and she tried to go twice more but was constrained by health issues. She maintained a strong relationship with several women in Kentucky who helped her a great deal as her illness progressed.

Dave

When I applied to transfer to Boston College after my sophomore year in college, I received a letter informing me that I was wait listed. I was disappointed and almost in tears. As soon as I left for work, Mom got on the phone with the admissions office. I am not exactly sure what she said but shortly thereafter I was notified that while I could not gain admission in the fall semester, I had been accepted for the spring semester. My move to BC was a life changing event.

Greg

Whenever we kids had a problem she always took the time to stop what she was doing and listen ... then give us her advice ... then dive in with both feet to help us solve the problem. As a result, it was not uncommon for her to engage with teachers, coaches and others on our behalf. We drew the line at her calling our bosses after we graduated from college. I don't think she ever called any of dad's bosses but I know she wanted to.

Dave

When our cousins moved from small towns north of Lockport to the big city of Rochester to attend St. John Fisher College, Mom made sure they had a home away from home at our house. They came often and brought many of their friends who also came to call her Aunt Patty. They said they came for her home cooking but I think it was for the laughs and motherly advice. Besides her thirty-four nieces and nephews, she is still affectionately known as Aunt Patty by a number of people met this way.

Greg

Mom was a nurse, but you would have thought she was a combination of the surgeon general and Dr. Phil. Everyone in the extended family called for advice with anything medical and she was frequently the "second opinion" family members sought out after a visit to the doctor. Most often her role was to reassure the caller that they would be okay or recommend an over the counter medicine or tell us kids, that we could not miss school for this ailment.

Dave

After her junior year in high school, when Aly's doctors told her she tore her ACL and would need surgery, Aly went on a mission to convince the doctors they were wrong. Dr. Mom somehow determined Aly's major concern was she did not want a big scar on her leg, after all her legs were her best feature. Dr. Mom promised plastic surgery could cover the scars but knew Aly would wear the scars as a badge of courage, which she still does today.

Greg

The cell phone was invented specifically with Mom and Aly in mind. They would talk several times a day whether they were a thousand miles apart or just down the street, sometimes I think they may have been in the same house. Mom would give advice on everything, sometimes unsolicited. Actually, mom reached out to anyone she cared about whenever she thought of them. No topic was out of bounds....I think this concerned Dad a lot!

Dave

Grandma Jean always said as a child Mom wore her emotions on her sleeve. She was the most sensitive of all eight siblings. She never tried to hide what she was feeling. She could laugh just as easily as she could cry. These traits served her well even as an adult. Maybe that's why she came across as so sincere with family and friends.

Greg's closing

Two very special lessons we will always remember from Mom were a part of the scripture reflection she gave at an Advent vesper service here at Transfiguration in December of 2004:

- It's okay to pray for the big miracles, but remember to be thankful for the small miracles the Lord brings to our lives every day
- Be careful to only measure what matters in your life.

We will miss you Mom. We know you are in a better place. You will always be with us. We will see you again when we all rest with God for eternity.

Next, the song "Angels Among Us" was played. Mike had told me that Patty wanted this song played because she felt that the FLOPS had been her Angels. However, I did not know the plan was to play it before I gave the reflection! This is a song that always makes Neil cry and I knew it was going to be difficult for me to speak after listening to it. So Neil quietly talked to me while it was playing so that we wouldn't listen to the words. I then got up to speak:

"Most of you have heard about the group of friends, neighbors and family called the FLOPS, who joined together to care for and support Patty. FLOPS stands for Friends and Loved Ones of Patty Stachura. Over and over Patty thanked us for what we were doing for her. We on the other hand, knew how much she was giving to us. I would like to share examples in five areas where our experience with Patty helped us to grow. Five areas that give another meaning to the word FLOPS.

First... the importance of Family and Friends. A small group grew to fifteen volunteers. This circle of friends became a community sharing our successes, vulnerabilities, tears and fears, all because Patty was willing to share hers with us. Sue shared, 'There are so few times in life, and maybe only once, that you meet someone who can affect your life so profoundly and for me it is Patty'. Another important friendship that the FLOPS felt truly blessed about was when Denise came into Patty's life as her Home Health

Aide. She joined the circle of friends and became a spiritual anchor for Patty.

In addition to friendship, Mike and Patty taught us the importance of our families and our marriages. Marital qualities such as dependence on each other, commitment, tenderness and patience were all demonstrated by 'St. Mike.' Patty demonstrated this family love by sharing herself with her kids in a special way. Last April she had a quilt made for each of them by Kim Cawley, which incorporated pictures of her with Dave, Aly and Greg. Patty personally chose the fabric and colors to be used and her own signature with love was in the center of each quilt taken from a card she had sent to Aly a long time ago. These were just recently given to the kids.

The second area was laughter, which was such an important part of our days. Playful banter was continuous. One FLOP gave Patty an appropriate nickname P.I.A., Pain in the (Ass). She earned this loving terminology by such things as making sure we spread the jelly to the very edges of her toast or comparing which of us made her soft boiled eggs exactly right. She would challenge us to keep up with her on walks by cranking the wheelchair speed up to the max. We razzed her that one day she wouldn't be able to yell at us. We decorated her wheelchair for Christmas. And even in her last week, I drew a smile from her when I arrived to stay with her one night wearing my nurses' cap and telling her the head nurse was here and wasn't taking any crap. Her beautiful eyes told us volumes: pain, laughter, tears and annoyance.

Ann reflected: 'the thing I think of most when I think of her is how she could roll her eyes and you knew exactly what she was trying to convey. They said mouthfuls.' If she said something I couldn't quite understand but acknowledged it as though I had, she would look me straight in the eye and say; *'OK, repeat it back to me!'* and the bluff was over! Bev said 'Your amazing humor warms my heart time and time again. Our friendship is the most treasured blessing in my entire life.'

The third thing she showed us was the importance of opportunity. Oh how she taught us to live each day and appreciate the precious gifts of life and living in the present. She helped us to see the beauty of each day by enjoying the cardinals at her feeders and the butterfly chrysalis she had in the kitchen. Because of Patty's example, we more fully treasure the opportunities we have to tell our children just how much we love them. She showed us how to use opportunities in life to set our priorities straight, God and family first above all else. Giving up her independence was likely the most difficult thing for Patty ... and yet even in that she taught us dignity and the lesson of trust. Lynn summed this up by writing to Patty, 'In your suffering we learned so much—that we all have crosses to bear; that you have to work hard at faith, friendships and other relationships; how to be better listeners, what is *really* important; how music and laughter are necessities, the importance of sisterhood, and how we can better live as God desires us to live and love'.

Our next and fourth lesson was in perseverance. In 2004, Patty was using a walker and sometimes a wheelchair. The need to rely on others for help was becoming more prevalent. She was determined to go on the women's retreat to Kentucky that spring just as she had many times before. And so she did. The result – a widening scope of friends who became the FLOPS, and the start of a weekly prayer group.

Jennifer reflected: 'Patty, Kentucky and prayer brought the FLOPS together. This loving and giving circle of friends is Patty's gift to us. This group of women is the real deal. We laugh, we cry, and we laugh some more. The bond is tight, the memories enduring. We are there for each other. We are all truly blessed to have been given the privilege of being a FLOP.' Kentucky held a special spot in Patty's life as did the cardinals that we continuously looked for as a sign of hope. From the beginning of our Kentucky trips we learned that to see a cardinal meant that all obstacles and concerns were going to be alright. Patty also had a fondness for butterflies relating to a story about her mother. As she became weaker I told her I had to ask a burning question… 'Am I looking for butterflies or cardinals as a sign of your nearness?' She smiled at me and said, *'Cardinals'*. As daily life became more difficult for her, Patty just tried harder. Eileen said, 'Patty's life while she was healthy and throughout her disease has been a lesson in grace, dignity, faith and courage.'

Her final gift to us was in her spirituality. Carol shared: 'the greatest gift was what came to be my absolute belief in God's promises of unconditional love, of forgiveness and of a life that never ends.' We learned how important God is in our lives on an everyday basis. But Patty didn't stop there. We also learned that it is OK to share our anger, frustration, and questions with Him as well. Our prayer group had lengthy discussions regarding the scripture where Jesus is asleep in the disciples' boat when a storm arises. Each of us admitted that at times it feels like Jesus is asleep in our boat. Patty was downright frank that she felt he was comatose in hers… and yet her trust in God was evident throughout this journey. This conversation went on for weeks.

Recently KC found an email from last January that

Patty sent regarding this discussion. In Patty's own words: 'Sometimes in the darkness I know He is there, but I forget to wake Him up. Somehow God always finds a way to help me feel and accept the changes happening to me. And I know for sure that not only is He beside me but He also gives me the miracle of friendship. Without that miracle every single day and all the joys, rays of hope and sometimes sadness that comes with it, He finds a way, through all of you to shine the light of hope upon me. There are no words to describe how grateful I am to have you all in my boat.'

And so now when you hear scriptures about being neighbor.... you will hopefully remember this true example. This past Wednesday morning our prayer group met around Patty's bedside to pray with her, not having done so in a month. It was very powerful and all I can say is that the room was filled with love and the Holy Spirit. I believe Patty was feeling welcomed into God's arms that morning and accepted his outstretched hand that very evening.

Family and Friends, Laughter, Opportunity, Perseverance and Spirituality. She touched us, she changed us and she will continue to be a part of us."

The service concluded with the song that had become known as the theme song of the FLOPS, "I Gave You Each Other" by Bob Schwartz.

Chapter 20

In the same way, let your light shine before men, that they may see your good deeds and praise your Father in heaven.

MATTHEW 5:16

During the days, weeks and months after Patty's death, her light continued to shine. The FLOPS felt rather lost at first as their day of the week rolled around with no purpose. But we had learned the importance of supporting each other and this we continued to do. The Wednesday prayer group carried on (and still does four years later) and has added new members who have experienced Kentucky and three who also lost their sister to ALS. We feel a reassurance that having once been her angels, Patty is now our angel and we call upon her frequently in times of need.

Mike found the house so empty, "This house is so full of Patty that it gets very difficult some days, but I don't want to change everything and take her out of our lives." Despite his sorrow, he was still able to give comfort to the wife of someone from Patty's ALS group who sent her condolences. His reply continued to be that of St. Mike:

"Thank you for your kind words. Patty was and is an inspiration for me. We learned a lot from her on this difficult journey and it has been my privilege to be her husband for 29 years.

This journey has been excruciating for me as her primary care giver. I feel all of her pain and anguish; I wanted to take it away but this disease just kept progressing. It's a very humbling and draining experience.

Barb, there are two things that kept me going especially the last very difficult year; our strong shared faith (and the support of our faith community) and a robust support system. There were a lot of people actively helping Patty, and therefore me, on this journey. Our support system included a very wonderful aide who became a great friend, Kim Cawley, who started out as our respiratory therapist but also became a great friend; the hospice nurse who in four weeks also became a great friend; our kids and several close friends who shouldered significant responsibility BUT gained from Patty much more than they gave.

Barb, keep your strength, you and Rick will need it. To quote Patty, 'Pray for the big miracle, the cure, but also be very aware of the little miracles that happen around you every day' (the friend who stops by just when you need them, the innocence of the grandkids when they stop over on a dark day, the wisdom of a friend, a rainbow or cardinal following a medical setback). If you would like to talk sometime in the future I'd be honored to share with you (and Rick) some of the things that we did to help both of us on this journey...but it will take me a week or so to get my head on straight first.

Remember, Job's journey was a difficult one as well, too. God bless you and Rick. He is watching over you!

Mike (& Patty)"

On November 1, just prior to Patty's death, Louise had sent an email to her: "My dear friend Patty, over the past years you've been such a big part of my life. I grew so fond of you. I'm selfish to say this, but I wish I'd known you sooner. Every butterfly, pretty flower and bird that I see, I say thank you Lord for all your little miracles, and thank you for my friend Patty. Please watch over her." At Easter 2009, Louise and Millard joined the Holy Family Catholic Church in Booneville. Mike traveled to Kentucky to be Louise's sponsor; seeds that had been sown were sprouting.

On November 10, the FLOPS received the following email from Peggy:

"Yesterday, my husband Peter emailed me the attached photo of his car mirror, which he took with his telephone camera. This happened more than once as the 'subject' kept returning to the car mirror. Peter clearly didn't know that it had significance but nevertheless thought it was very unusual. What can be said!? "

There were many other cardinal sightings by the FLOPS but not for me. It wasn't until New Year's Day that Patty finally made herself known to me. But the most spectacular sighting was yet to come. Dave and Ericka were married on May 12, 2007 at the Church of the Transfiguration. Outdoor pictures were being taken at the reception venue and Mike was milling around outside waiting for his turn. And then he saw them – a male and female cardinal just sitting and watching the activities. This news spread quickly through the FLOPS as one more affirmation that Patty was indeed present at this occasion.

Patty's ashes were laid to rest on January 27, 2007 in a small private service with Fr. Mike Bausch presiding at the graveside. It was a simple but emotional ceremony. After Fr. Mike had completed the service and the readings accompanying it, K.C. asked him to read the Gospel scripture for the Mass of the day. It was the story of Jesus in the Boat! I don't believe that Fr. Mike had any idea what the significance was, but most of those present did!

Before beginning to write this book, K.C. and I sat with Denise and asked her to talk about some of her memories with Patty. One of those memories was reading Bible passages to her. She said that Patty especially liked Psalm 27 and Psalm 37. As I sat going through old emails while writing this chapter, I came across the email that K.C. had sent with the Bible readings for the last Prayer service we had with Patty on November 8th. The Responsorial Psalm for that day was taken from Psalm 27. That chapter sounded somewhat familiar to me and so I had to go back and check my notes from Denise. I was simply amazed by the significance. It reads:

Responsorial Psalm Ps 27:1, 4, 13-14

R. (1a) **The Lord is my light and my salvation.**

The LORD is my light and my salvation; whom should I fear? The LORD is my life's refuge; of whom should I be afraid?

R. **The Lord is my light and my salvation.**

One thing I ask of the LORD; this I seek: To dwell in the house of the LORD all the days of my life, That I may gaze on the loveliness of the LORD and contemplate his temple.

R. **The Lord is my light and my salvation.**

I believe that I shall see the bounty of the LORD in the land of the living. Wait for the LORD with courage; be stouthearted, and wait for the LORD.

R. **The Lord is my light and my salvation.**

Talk about being welcomed by the Lord! Again, there are no coincidences in life; God's hand is in everything.

K.C. had several revelations as well, "As you know, I have had several dreams that seemed very, very, real with Patty as the lead actress." An email from January 2007: "I had quite the dream last night. It was the first one since she died and it was very clear. At first I was 'working' at the house getting ready...and then she was walking to the front door (and talking, I might add!) Somehow it was apparent that she was coming home from the hospital and her comments were *'The new legs will work better in a couple of days, I'm still stiff'* and something else about *'Thanks for doing so much to get the house ready'.*"

A week later K.C. had another dream: "Patty was walking around and having some difficulty with her foot but she made some comment about *'it's much better than it was when I couldn't walk!'* There was also a dream about Forest Hills and having lunch there with her when I said that I was so glad that she could finally sit next to me again instead of at the end of the table (with the wheelchair). She commented: *'Of course you know that I will always be sitting next to you'.* So I am not sure what to make of this, except that I feel somewhat privileged to even dream about her."

Do any of us really know what dreams signify? Throughout both the Old and New Testaments of the Bible, scripture reveals the many visions and dreams that came from God. Their symbolism brought those fortunate enough to receive them to a deeper faith. Perhaps that is all we need to understand.

Aly and Scott Yoder were married June 29, 2007 in Canandaigua and had a lovely outdoor reception without a nudist in sight! They chose to dance their wedding dance to

"I Gave You Each Other." There were a lot of tissues being used. Patty now has two grandsons, William Edward Yoder born September 26, 2008 and Chase Michael Yoder born September 10, 2010. After William was born, Aly and Scott received a wall hanging Patty had bought for the occasion. Mike declares, "Grandchildren are a blast!"

The FLOPS gathered for prayer at Patty's graveside on the first anniversary of her death, November 8, 2007. The readings were: Romans 14:7-12; Psalm 27:1, 4, 13-14 (AGAIN) and the Gospel was taken from Luke 15:1-10. I did a short reflection relating these passages to music since it had been so important to the FLOPS.

> "All three readings today allude to the principle of putting God first in our lives since each of us will be held accountable to Him when we meet Him face to face. I love this reading from Romans – 'For it is written: As surely as I live, says the Lord, every knee will bow before me; every tongue will confess to God.' (Romans 14:11) —because I love the song, 'I Can Only Imagine'. I can just picture Patty standing, kneeling, dancing, praising and singing before the Lord. It is a glorious image as we remember our friend and how she touched each of our hearts to grow closer to God.
>
> I was always taught that the Psalms were like poetry or songs and so a few different ones from my childhood came to mind. You know.... those Protestant songs such as 'I Believe', 'It is No Secret', and 'Surely Goodness and Mercy'. I think that through all of our days with Patty we found how meaningful music became for us. Now, many

songs I listen to bring her very close to my heart and spirit as I am sure the same happens with each of you.

I had a harder time sensing a particular song when I read the Gospel. However, an immediate image came to me of sitting and reading this Bible story about the lost sheep to my son Adam when he was about 18 months old; how excited he would get at the end of the book when he could 'find the sheep'. I was drawn to the last sentence of the gospel, 'In the same way, I tell you, there is rejoicing in the presence of the angels of God over one sinner who repents.' (Luke 15:10) Can't you just see Patty as one of the angels rejoicing with God over one sinner repenting? I can also hear her saying 'What took you so long!' I finally was drawn to the song 'Angels Among Us' because Patty had a unique way of bringing us together, showing us love, lighting our way to draw us closer in our faith and teaching us how to help each other in the years to come. Yes, Lord, she was a pretty powerful influence in our lives."

The Wednesday Prayer Group and FLOPS had gathered at the Stachura home since 2004 to bake Christmas cookies early in December. These were mornings filled with fun and laughter and even though Patty could not physically make cookies, she certainly was able to direct how to decorate them from her chair! The fun continued since you never knew if everyone was going to bring the same cookie dough, to sending Hutch on a mission in the basement to find whiskey for Irish coffee. True to form, Mike invited the group that December after Patty died to come to the house to make cookies. We think he was afraid that he and Greg might not get any if we baked elsewhere! The FLOPS were a bit reflective that year. Then K.C. went home and read the following calendar meditation for the day, "Praise be to the ... God of all comfort, who comforts us in all our troubles, so that we can comfort those in any trouble with the comfort we ourselves have received from God. 2 Corinthians 1: 3-4." Her comment, "And who says there isn't more than just 'cookie comfort' going on today??"

But the following year (2007) was even more notable as she sent this email to me while I was living in England. "I forgot to tell you this about Wednesday at cookie baking. Bill tried to call me and just opened our phone book and dialed the Stachura number. (He is not up on cell phone prefixes.) Total surprise when Patty's voice came on the phone with her message! Jolted, he then called the real Stachura land line and explained to me who he had just 'talked' to. See, I know she is trying to be ET and phone home to let us know she is OK! Mike explained that the contract has not run out on her phone yet. It was a teary announcement to everyone that day that Bill had just talked to Patty!"

Once again, Mike was asked to give an Advent reflection in December 2007 at the Church of the Transfiguration. I have included part of this reflection.

READING: *1 Thessalonians 5:19-24*

A reading from Paul's first letter to the Thessalonians

> Do not put out the Spirit's fire; do not treat prophecies with contempt, Test everything; Hold on to the good. Avoid every kind of evil. May God

himself, the God of peace, sanctify you through and through. May your whole spirit, soul, and body be kept blameless at the coming of our Lord Jesus Christ. The one who calls you is faithful and he will do it.

"Just about three years ago, my wife Patty and I had the privilege to co-lead Advent Evening Prayer. I read the scripture passage and Patty gave the reflection. I think the scripture passage tonight builds perfectly on her reflection. It had been a year since she was diagnosed with ALS and her life, *our lives,* was changing. Her reflection centered around two points:

- First, dismiss your anxiety, give over to God your problems and concerns, then trust in His great fatherly love.

- Second, measure what matters in your preparation for Advent and in life. What mattered to her were faith, family, and friends.

The scripture passage this evening calls us to test everything and live life to the fullest but only retain what is good. As we live life, nurture the Spirit and prophecies, and avoid evil.

I have learned over the last three years that my life on this earth is a special gift from our loving Father. I have the opportunity every day to enjoy life, live it to the fullest and experience His great love in many ways. We find Him in the beauty of nature. We find Him in all people but especially in the relationships we have with someone special: family, friends, and a colleague.

I have learned that experiencing God in the beauty of nature does not require climbing Mt. Everest or hiking through Mendon Ponds Park. It could, but it does not have to. It could be simply appreciating the sunset. It could be seeing a caterpillar hatch into a butterfly or watching through the window at the cardinals feeding, or evening primrose flowering in your yard and knowing that these are all gifts from God.

I have learned that experiencing God in our special personal relationships does not require a special event or place. For that matter it does not require anything special. It might simply be a conversation over a cup of coffee. It might be a short telephone call just to let someone know you care, that they are special to you. But it does not even really require the ability to talk; just the opportunity to be there for one another. Truly BE THERE, not because you need to be there, but because you want to be there, appreciating the other for simply who they are.

I have had the opportunity to truly live life. This journey has been different—with Patty before things were complicated by ALS, with her on her journey with the disease, and more recently traveling this journey without my soul mate. I do believe that God calls us to live and enjoy life. But I have found it is equally important to, in the words of St Paul:

- retain only what is good
- and avoid evil.

It's too easy to live life FOR ME and not FOR GOD. It's too easy for ego, desire, and for pleasure to distract us. After all we are human.

As I journeyed with Patty, I had the opportunity to see just how meaningless material treasures really are. Not that they are bad, or evil, but in the grand scheme of things they just are not that important...."

Several of the FLOPS drew strength from sharing in Patty's journey as they lost other loved ones. Sue, who had never experienced the death of someone close, lost her father. She told me that she was able to bear the grief because she had walked Patty's journey with her. Jo-Ellen lost her mother after a brief illness. Her mother's last days were not peaceful. The power of prayer, magnified during Patty's journey gave strength and solutions to Jo-Ellen during those difficult hours. While I was living in London, my mother, who had been quite healthy, had an unexpected mishap and died suddenly. The faith that had intensified as a FLOP led me to declare that God is still merciful and to know in my heart that she was never alone as Patty was right there with her.

Greg and Sara Beth have just started their lives together, having married on August 1, 2009. Patty would be so happy that "her baby" was finally married! Greg and SB incorporated several touches into their special day as a remembrance to Patty. The morning began with Greg, Dave and Mike visiting the cemetery and then to Forest Hills for breakfast. Before Sara Beth walked down the aisle, Greg, Aly, and Dave lit a memorial candle for their mother which was prominently displayed on the altar. A special touch at the reception included Greg and Aly dancing together to "I Gave You Each Other" for what typically would have been the mother's dance.

As at Dave and Aly's weddings, there was also a remembrance table at the reception with pictures of Patty with the family and ALS bracelets for guests to take. The day after each wedding, the kids received through Mike the cross and card that Patty and Lynn had purchased for them for their special day.

So Patty certainly lives on in our hearts and memories, and she not only taught us about struggle but also about hope. Joan Chitister explains, "Struggle not only transforms us, it makes us transforming as well. (Hope) is about becoming open to the God of newness. It is about allowing ourselves to let go of the present (and) to believe in the future we cannot see but can trust to God." [19]

Epilogue

I am the vine; you are the branches.
If a man remains in me and I in him, he will bear much
fruit; apart from me you can do nothing.
This is to my Father's glory, that you bear much fruit,
showing yourselves to be my disciples.

JOHN 15: 5, 8

My family lived on a farm in Ohio when I was growing up. My brother and I would often play in the
woods with two neighbor kids. We would swing on the wild
grapevines over a shallow creek, knowing that we would
be scolded (or worse) if we fell in and came home with wet
and muddy shoes and clothes. We trusted that those vines
would hold our weight. What imagery this verse invokes in
me of trusting Jesus to hold us as we swing over the often
deep chasms of life. We have no way of knowing if we will
be able to swing to the other side; faith and trust in God
must persevere if we are to face these many challenges.
Patty started out swinging over puddles, but through this
three-year journey her leap of faith allowed her to face the
Grand Canyon.

Not only does this chapter of John reaffirm our trust in Jesus as the vine, but he specifically tells us that we are the branches, branches that are continuously pruned to yield a bigger crop. Barb also addressed this scripture verse in her 2000 Kentucky reflection. "We learned that if we remain attached to Christ's vine, letting his love flow through us, that everything will be OK. Today the vine who is Jesus continues to grow, to branch out, and to bear fruit in us all. It is our challenge to remain united to him and to one another; to be pruned by his Word by sharing in the cross so as to bear the fruit that will feed our (spiritually) hungry, starving world."

I can see the analogy of Patty and the FLOPS as the pruned branches bearing fruit. By staying focused and connected to Christ, Patty allowed Him to strip her of things such as fear, vanity, doubt, and apathy in order to touch so many lives. "Pruning" these things from our lives helps prepare us to be His disciples and to bring forth His love to others.

"You did not choose me, but I chose you and appointed you to go and bear fruit—fruit that will last. Then the Father will give you whatever you ask in my name. This is my command: Love each other." (John 15:16) God uses many ways to converse with us; this verse at Sunday Mass empowered me to concentrate on the ending of the FLOPS story. What was the significance of Patty's journey and the relationship that each of the FLOPS experienced with her? Why were we chosen? As the prior chapter mentions, there were many things that happened in the months after Patty died. Jennifer once said, "Patty brought us together." A group of 'Pittsford women', who Patty previously felt would never accept her, became her angels. A body that she at one time was ashamed of became unimportant as she found

God changing her from within. Her journey, though tragic, wasn't for naught. She taught us to live in the moment and savor each blessing no matter how small. She showed us how to be friends to each other and support each other. All of us were touched in differing ways.

- **Allyson** - "My personal gift from Patty's experience was the depth of the friendship that developed as a result of her sharing the progressive surrender of all that she hated losing with a group of women; some of whom were on a similar road to realizing that life truly does not hold the security of entitlement. The connection transcended all the Pittsford-isms that she so hated. However difficult her entire journey, she shared her discovery of that lesson with everyone in an open and, many times, very raw manner. Her example taught me to speak for myself and let the emotions fly once in awhile. I came away from those years totally different from what I could have been when my life, as I knew it, fell to pieces. She cared so deeply for so many of us and expressed it readily; we came out way ahead as a result."

- **Lynn** – "I probably learned more about how to be a better mother from her in those two-and-one-half years than in the previous thirteen! The stories she shared (while never betraying her kids' privacy) revealed her and her family's struggles and resolutions. I keep hearing and sharing her stories and subtle advice even though her voice is now quiet."

- **Sue** – "There are so many things that have so much more meaning since being her friend. When I see a butterfly or pass Powder Mill Park, or put jelly on toast, just the way she wanted it, I can smile and be grateful for her deep presence that will always be in my heart. I feel very blessed to have acquired so many wonderful friends all because our dear Patty had to suffer with a most horrible disease."

- **K.C.** – "From this experience I know that we must feed our friendships to make them grow and flourish (and NO, not just with breakfast and lunch stops along the way!). You can't expect friendships to grow if they are not weeded and fertilized. Yes, I said weeded – there has to be hard times to make the participants stronger; and somehow we come out of it with smoother edges and a brighter future for having known each other." Her other reflection: "I have come to the conclusion that it was GRACE that Patty was serving each one of us. We learned grace from her and from each other and we showed our grace to her and to others. The definition of grace by the way:
  - the freely given, unmerited favor and love of God.
  - the influence or spirit of God operating in humans to regenerate or strengthen them.
  - a virtue or excellence of divine origin: the Christian graces."

- **Eileen** – "The biggest impact that she has had on me over the past seventeen years is the priorities she and Mike had in the way they lived their life and raised their family. Money, prestige and pretense were not on their list of things to worry about. Their example and support has been very influential on Brian and me. If I were to describe her it would be as a tireless mother and wife, daughter, sister and true friend."

- **Carol** – "Her concern for others was always present, deflecting attention away from herself. She shared great parenting advice and offered me support when she was dependent on me to wipe her nose. Her incredible journey to the end of her life helped me to value the precious gift of life, of breathing deeply, of gliding through water, or still being able to put my own socks on even if my back hurts, to appreciate the gift of being present in the moment even by taking two hours to really try to understand the depth and feelings she tried to convey, right to the last time I saw her. She had a beautiful smile that responded to even the most ridiculous jokes. Perhaps the greatest gift that I received from Patty was what came to be my own absolute belief in God's promises— of unconditional love, of forgiveness, of a life that never ends. It was my most fervent prayer for Patty that she would feel God rocking her boat and hold tight to the knowledge that she was never alone and is, and always has been, wrapped in his loving embrace."

- **Peggy** – "Patty was so soulfully caring of her family and friends. She was a very strong and opinionated advocate for what she held dear and yet she completely lacked self-confidence. It's ironic but not surprising, that she gained a strong and abiding faith and self-confidence as she faced up to her illness and imminent death. I truly believe that this courage in large part came from her relationship with her wonderful Mike. Together they unknowingly set the example for the rest of us … an extraordinary couple who braved life and death together. That is what has influenced me the most about the Patty and Mike story."

- **Cindi Newman** –"I didn't meet Patty or the other FLOPS until she was wheelchair bound. She was almost always full of humor, even when she wrestled with the deep issues of her prognosis. Though the disease was crueler than any other I had witnessed, I had not seen a clearer manifestation of the love of God among any group of people. The FLOPS stood together unified in their purpose, solid in their desire to walk with Patty through whatever came. As Patty's body degenerated, the body of Christ, through the FLOPS, was being built up and strengthened. For me, to have had the privilege of joining them in that journey is beyond words. I cannot thank God enough for these women who modeled the heart of God with a faithful and steadfast presence in Patty's daily life. As her needs increased, so increased the efforts of the FLOPS...daily meals for over two years, housecleaning, driving, someone always with her. I will never view God's love the same way after experiencing the miracle we all shared during Patty's journey home ... and Patty was always at the center of it all. She was worth every moment!!"

- **Barbara** – "She touched me with her love of life; I remember her blowing bubbles at (my daughter) Lori's wedding before she was diagnosed. In fact she had fallen for the first time, just the week before, but she made it to the wedding anyway. Knowing Patty, loving Patty has made me a better person. Watching her in the final weeks of her life taught me how life should be lived with faith and love and always with a smile on your lips. I gave her an assignment when she met our Lord, and I know that she has done it. I owe my weight loss to her; she spoke about going to Weight Watchers and how she had worked so hard. So the January after she died I went to WW, for me but also for her too, as a testament to her. Patty truly changed my life."

- **Jennifer** – "My journey with Patty taught me how I had to change. I was selfish and superficial. I couldn't and wouldn't enter into her pain. I tried to keep things light and upbeat by telling her stories to keep her amused and distracted....to keep from talking about the elephant in the room. I didn't know Patty very well when I became a FLOP and if I could keep from knowing her; maybe it would hurt less when she died. I cheated us both. I hope I've learned to become real and present. I wish I could do it all over again."

- **Sis** – "I was impacted most by the love and devotion of all the other FLOPS. They taught me a great deal!"

- **Bev** - "Each day something seems to happen that makes me think of Patty. The highlight of my week was to be there with her. She exemplified courage in many ways. She bravely faced her circumstances and disease as well as courageously opening herself up to FLOPS like me that she didn't know very well. Through it all, she never forgot how to laugh and to make others laugh. It was a joy to be with her. I continue to admire her, and am encouraged by her example to face my own challenges. Patty is a cherished blessing in my life and I will forever hold her close in heart, soul and mind. I deeply miss our dear Patty."

- **Becky** – "No matter how restricted she became in her activities there was always that enthusiasm to continue as normal a life as possible. What a spirit! Her desire was like a bright burning candle that would emanate light (God's light), and be an example for all of us. I simply marveled at her acceptance of what God placed before her. There had to be an energy there that could only be given to her by God. Through all of this there radiated a love for what she did even in her suffering."

- **Connie** – "The journey of Patty and the FLOPS was like a trip to the top of a rough, icy, steep mountain that also harbored a few lush valleys where Patti's agony (journey) helped others."

- **Jo-Ellen** – "The FLOPS experience was life changing for me. I was previously in a career which had a limited range of interaction with others. After witnessing Patty's courage, love, and outreach in helping others with ALS, I realized she was a true, living example of Christ. Being with Patty fostered my emotional growth, maturity, and understanding of how to be present for others. It brought active listening and laughter to care giving. Her friendship in unity with the FLOPS was both a blessed experience and inspiration for my new direction in the health care field."

- **Ann** – "I appreciated her humanness, annoyance, frustration, strength (not by choice), resistance to change, love of food, family, and good times."

- **Joan** – "I was touched by how much concern Patty showed to me when I was diagnosed with lymphoma in 2006. She so easily looked outside her own problems to worry about me by calling and sending cards. It is truly a gift to be able to put others ahead of you and Patty would often do this."

- **Karen** – "Patty modeled courage and resilience for us. She fought to live every moment of each day the best she could. At times she seemed to be barely hanging on by her fingernails, and yet she continued on down the path because there was nothing else to do. Her deep faith and relationship with God brought her through some dark nights; sometimes she walked with God and other times she would say, *God carried me.*"

- **As for Myself** – "I can't begin to explain the overwhelming evidence of God's love and His very existence that I now really see each day. Despite other painful losses, I know that God is good. I treasure the little things in life so much more….the exquisiteness of a flower, a phone call from my daughter, playful bantering with my son, holding my husband's hand, a letter from a friend, the beautiful vistas that I have experienced all over the world and the simple words I love you."

Patty and Mike demonstrated faith, trust, and love. The courage they illustrated provides us with courage to draw on in our own lives. The FLOPS have modeled how a group of believers can come together to form a community and change lives; their story has touched many people. None of the FLOPS will ever be the same again. In this respect, Patty's journey truly was a victory.

I think that as a group, the FLOPS would all agree that through this experience we were called to bear witness (fruit) to God; to give away what we received. To quote Barb's Kentucky homily of 2000, "as believers we are all united or intertwined; and as believers we are invited to love, not in word or speech, but in truth or action." This experience has given us a new understanding of what it means to love your neighbor (Matthew 22:36-40). What an honor it has been for us to be chosen for this task.

$\mathcal{NOTES}$

All scripture quotations, unless otherwise indicated, are taken from the Holy Bible, New International Version®. Copyright ©1973, 1978, 1984 by International Bible Society. Used by permission of International Bible Society.

1. "Change." By permission. From *Merriam-Webster's Collegiate® Dictionary, 11th Edition*©2009 by Merriam-Webster, Incorporated (www.Merriam-Webster.com).

2. Chittister, Joan D. *Scarred by Struggle, Transformed by Hope.* (Grand Rapids, MI.: William B. Erdmans Publishing Co., 2003), p. 19

3. "State and County QuickFacts: Owsley County, Kentucky." *U.S. Census Bureau.* 02 December 2010. http://quickfacts. census.gov/qfd/states/21/21189.html

4. Virtue, Doreen. *Healing With Angels Oracle Cards.* (Carlsbad, CA.: Hay House, Inc., 1999), p. 12

5. ALS Division Muscular Dystrophy Association. *Facts About Amyotrophic Lateral Sclerosis.* P. 9

6. Chittister, p. 28.

7. Robin L. Flanigan. "Her Help Comes From All Sides." *Rochester Democrat and Chronicle.* www.democratand-chronicle.com. 8 June 2005. p. 1C, 6C

8. "Kübler-Ross model." *Wikipedia, The Free Encyclopedia.* 5 Jul 2009, 04:32 UTC. 5 Jul 2009 http://en.wikipedia. org/w/index.php?title=K%C3%BCbler-Ross_ model&oldid=300350137 .

9. "Meditation," *The Word Among Us*, 26 September 2008, p. 46.

10. Chittister, p. 22

11. Krause, Frank. "My Dad's Love." *Thoughts About God*. Np. 4 August 2008. http://www.thoughts-about-god.com/stories/krause_f.htm

12. Shrader, Bertie. "Stranger in the House." *The Word Among Us*. Easter 2008. p. 68

13. *The Word Among Us*. January 2006. np

14. "Faith". By permission. From *Merriam-Webster's Collegiate® Dictionary, 11th Edition©2009* by Merriam-Webster, Incorporated (www.Merriam-Webster.com).

15. St. Augustine. *Book of Famous Quotes*. 8 April 2008. http://www.famous-quotes.com/author.php?aid=338

16. Salzberg, Sharon. Inspirational and Motivational Quotes: E-H. *Choice Quotations*. 14 July 2009. p 3. http://choicequotations.com/motivational-inspirational-3.html

17. Ward, Georgia. Quotes in paragraph taken from notes in her personal journal. 8 August 2008.

18. Buber, Martin. *Good Reads*. 24 June, 2010. http://www.goodreads.com/author/quotes/29357.Martin_Buber

19. Chittister, p. 100

For additional information on Amyotrophic Lateral Sclerosis, also known as ALS, Lou Gehrig's Disease or Motor Neuron Disease, please see the following websites:

http://www.alsa.org

http://www.als-mda.org/disease/als.html

Breinigsville, PA USA
17 February 2011
255780BV00001B/2/P